THE PHOTON FIELD

The Twelve Days of Light

PROPHECY CONCERNING THE MILLENNIUM

Gary Bonnell, Ph.D.

Richman Rose Publishing • Atlanta, Georgia

The Twelve Days of Light
Prophecy Concerning the Millennium

Copyright © 1998 by Gary Bonnell

ISBN # 1-879604-12-4
Library of Congress Catalog Number: 98-65185

Printed in the United States of America

Richman Rose Publishing
PO Box 7766
Atlanta, Georgia 30357-0766

Photography: front cover image copyright © 1998 PhotoDisc, Inc.
Cover Design, Illustrations & Page Layout: Gary Bonnell
Editing & Proofreading: Kathleen Pringle

Also by Gary Bonnell

ASCENSION The Original Teachings of Christ Awareness

YOUR BOOK OF LIFE Accessing the Akashic Records

This book is not intended for everyone.

It is intended for those who have incarnated with the Knowing of fifth-dimensional awareness, whether they are immediately conscious of it or not. This is a guide to understanding the subtle layers of circumstance that are about to overtake human consciousness so that they might demonstrate at the highest level the new order of conditions concerning this realm.

"If I speak in the tongues of men
and of angels,
but have not love,
I am a noisy gong or a clanging cymbal.
And if I have prophetic powers,
and understand
all the mysteries and all
the knowledge, and if I
have all faith, so as to move mountains,
but have not love,
I am nothing.
If I give away all I have, and if I deliver
my body to be burned,
but have not love,
I gain nothing."

Corinthians 13: 1

INTRODUCTION

The information presented in this work is a compilation of data collected from private Akashic readings over a period of ten years. Once the event of the Twelve Days was revealed through these private sessions, detailed information about the Twelve Days of Light was received directly from the Akasha without going through the filtering hopes and dreams of clients. This resulted in a greater clarity about the overall pattern of energy emanating from the center of Creation that so profoundly effects every moment of our existence here in the physical realms.

In this presentation each of the Twelve Days is detailed to give a full understanding of the transformation of consciousness as we enter the next paradigm. This shift happens every thirteen thousand years creating an alternating cycle of unity and separation. This is a multiverse event and effects all consciousness equally, no matter the form of dimensional manifestation. An individual can be in the etheric field of the planet and still undergo the shift to unity. This bears repeating: being on terra ferma is not required to move into unity.

There is a group on the planet who would stop the shift to unity, primarily because they have acquired a taste for the energy released when consciousness experiences sorrow. We cannot alter the immutable nature of this event any more than we could stop the Earth from turning. It is because of this that the outcome will be determined at the response level. Therefore, your response to this thirteen thousand year event will ultimately determine the balance of your existence here on Earth, or elsewhere. Because response is so important, three basic response scenarios (page 29) are scripted as a way of illustrating the three basic extremes that will play out in the Western collective mind. The scripts are a form of outcome imaging designed to help fill in the details at a personal level of the beginning moments of this cosmic event.

The timing of this event was a little confusing as first, mainly because of the four year discrepancy between actual dating and the Gregorian calendar. Fortunately, the Akasha is a living data system that allows for such a discrepancy by adjusting itself to the dominate illusionary understanding of time.

Then there was the very annoying presentation of near identical sound symbols in the Akasha for the genesis of the Aquarian Age, which the Twelve Days of Light heralds. Each time the Akashic Records are asked to present an exact time, two date are given – 2001 and 2011. Because the Akasha groups like data streams, no one can be one hundred percent sure if the dates given are separate events or beginning and ending dates of a duration. The chapter on timing (page 1) covers this in more detail.

The fact that a collectively defining moment is upon us, whether it is one event of two, or is over a period of time, is neither here nor there. The good news is that we have readied ourselves through our many incarnations since the last event of this magnitude back in Atlantis. There is only one thing left to do – release our deep inner conflict. The energy of the Twelve Days will greatly magnify individual consciousness. This magnification of conflict is the judgement so many past prophets saw in their visions of tribulation. Individual conflict creates stress; stress creates disease; disease destroys the structures of the physical body. If enough individuals are in deep conflict the structures of the collective mind will be destroyed. Profound conflict is the current state of the collective mind. It appears it will self destruct in favor of a new form.

The information presented here is given as an aid to those wishing to take this opportunity to step outside the collective mind, off the ancient wheel of birth and death, out of the conflict of duality and into the sovereignty of Creation.

Gary Bonnell
Atlanta, Georgia

TABLE of CONTENTS

TIMING

"And a great portent appeared in the heaven, a woman clothed with the sun, with the moon under her feet, and on her head a crown of twelve stars; she was with child and she cried out in her pangs of birth, in her anguish for delivery."
— Revelation: 12: 1

At the end of the last millennium a great number of people in Europe did not plant crops or put up winter stores because they believed it to be the end time when the faithful would be caught up into heaven in the rapture. Needless to say, in the first year of the next millennium those same individuals experienced lean times. Many actually starved to death. At every hundred year mark since, there has been an outcry of the prophesied end times.

If there is to be a second coming of Christ, or an apocalypse, then the single most important question other than why, would be, when?

Timing in all prophecy is difficult. Not because it is impossible to determine, but because of the complexity of the concept of time itself.

On the other side of the veil, in the region of consciousness where the Akasha is constantly being created, time as we experience it does not exist. Instead, the units of measure are more like sacred geometric forms (markers) that build at intersecting points of awareness where agreements of senses meet in great moments of expansion and contraction. These moments of expansion and contraction create the multidimensional markers the collective mind uses to perceive its growth. These moments are not linear, but simultaneous, including all the markers associated with each intersecting point of awareness. Every event in the Akasha is shown to be interconnected with all events, from the beginning to the end. These shared moments of dimensional awareness are the foundation of the multiverse (as opposed to universe) calendar displayed in the Akasha. Because of this, no date is singularly expressed. In our world we look along an imaginary line into the past or future from a beginning point. The only beginning point in the Akasha is "THE" beginning point, of which there is only one, and it includes the ending moment as well. This is confusing only because we are accustomed to linear time. Our only point of experience that comes close to this type of time awareness is our dream state.

If you ask the Akasha to reveal the exact moment in which a single event is to take place, you will be given a series of sound symbols that look something like this:

Hidden in this series of symbolic sound forms are the dates 2001 and 2011. This is the answer I received when stating, "Reveal for Knowing the moment the collective mind shifts to fifth-dimensional awareness?"

Seldom have I ever gotten two dates as the answer to a stated intention. Being of human consciousness, I naturally want to interpret the two dates to represent the beginning and ending moments in the collective shift from third/fourth-dimensional awareness to fifth-dimensional mind. The logic of this realm seldom ever applies to the reality on the other side of the veil. When I asked for greater clarity, I got a more refined same answer:

 A    B

The symbols in illustration A are used to express the exact moment of the millennium shift, but still include both dates 2001 and 2011. At least here the month of July is given for 2001 and the month of December is given for 2011. But still the problem remains: are the dates a beginning and ending period, or are they two separate possible dates for the same event? Asking for greater clarity only gets the same answer in more minute detail as seen in the illustration B.

The symbols at the top of the next page represent both years 2001 and 2011 respectively. The difference being in the beginning sound markers of each date as indicated below:

 As best as can be determined, the difference between the two dates is in the two dots above the center line in one date and below in another.

To solve the problem of whether these symbols represent a beginning and ending moment, or two different beginning dates, I turned to more worldly means.

Our calendars are used to string together moments of "reality" to give a sequence to seemingly related events. Because there is no calendar per say in the Akashic Records, just a series of symbols representing sounds that express moments of expansion and contraction within and around the collective mind, I turned to documents here in this realm, blending information from both realities to form the final interpretation of the timing.

The Akashic Records indicate seven two thousand year cycles when referencing the Twelve Days of Light event itself. The Twelve Days happen at the very center of the thousand year thick wave – from the center of one wave to the center of the next is fourteen thousand years – five hundred years on either side of the thirteen thousand year interval.

a) In the Akashic Records it indicates that the pyramid attributed to Cheops was designed and built by the Atlantans as a calendar to measure the thirteen thousand year intervals between the thousand year thick energy events that alter consciousness here on Earth. In measuring the stones from the entrance of the pyramid to the middle of the King's Chamber, (giving each stone an equivalent of one hundred years) we crossed the half way point in approximately 5000BCE. The leading edge of this current wave overtook us five hundred years ago. That puts us at the center of this one thousand year wave.

(Note: In his book, *"Pyramid Odyssey,"* W. R. Fix elaborates about how the pyramids were used as units of measure to determine the mas of the Earth and its exact cycles between the great shift points that so greatly effect humankind.)

> b) Edgar Cayce calculates each cycle to be approximately 12,500 years in duration. He places the final destruction of Atlantis at the end of the third world age in 9600BCE. That corresponds to the Records account of the <u>final</u> breakup of Atlantis. Cayce goes on to speculate that the fourth world age will last until 1998-2001CE. (The Akashic records indicate enormous change between July of 1999 and May of 2000. This is right in the middle of the Cayce prediction window.)
> c) In astrology the term "Great Year" is equal to one astrological month, or two thousand years. The Piscean Age began with the appearance of Jeshua ben Joseph and ends with the coming of, "The Great Friend," in 2000CE as foretold by Guatama Siddartha, the Buddha, in 484BCE. Buddha gave this bringer of light the name "Maitreya."
> Buddha believed that every twenty-five hundred years marks the end of one age and the beginning of another. Buddha was born at the beginning of the last great cycle in the year 560BCE.
> d) Another manner used to determine the timing is the five thousand year cycles used by the Buddhists. This present cycle is Aryan Kali Yuga which ends in the year 2000CE.

The only culture to indicate the shifting of human consciousness out of time, and therefore into the fifth-dimensional awareness, were the Myans. They put this event in 2012 on the winter solstice. The Akasha indicates this as the moment when <u>all</u> human consciousness steps out of time as a limitation or boundary. With all other writings indicating the 2000 - 2001 period as the moment of shift in the collective, I feel certain as to the two dates being given as a window of opportunity that spans the beginning for individuals and end for the collective mind. While it is true that the en masse shift will happen between 2001-2011, it is also true that each individual will have their own experience of the exact timing of their shift to fifth-dimensional awareness. And there is enough energy present now to individually shift. Everyone will be aware of at least the first two days of the Twelve Days of Light.

The common citizens of Europe in the year 999CE did not have access to all these other prophecies. They only had the interpretations of their deliverance minded clergy to guide them. Had circumstances allowed them this current knowledge, they might have planted crops.

By as best as can be determined, we, the whole lot of us, are at the time of Revelation.

To some this carries the harrowing promise of tribulation and pestilence, while others find within the visions of what is to come, a greater experience for humankind. Unfortunately, most of the documented visions of this end time period, ranging from the Old Testament prophets Isaiah and Ezekeil, to modern seers, such as Nostradamus or even more recently, Edgar Cayce, point to the destruction of the old system without giving a clear vision of the expansion and joy of the new paradigm. This in no way means these individuals could only see the negative circumstantial aspects of this period; it simply indicates the need to know within the present collective mind the worst possible scenario. This is symptomatic of the learning though hardship mind set of the Picean age. The Aquarian age of self-realization that quickly follows this coming period of upheaval ushers in the unification of body, mind and spirit, allowing us the ability to envision a reality free of struggle and strife.

The phenomenon of prophecy is flawed in that it is filtered through the dominate cultural beliefs and language of a given time or age. Science fiction writers have an easier time articulating the future because they are free to elaborate on their visions without concern for how it will be received. It is because of this "no investment in the accuracy" posture that many have gotten very close to the actual happenings of the period being speculated. The most tainting of all personality filters in the art of prophecy is the need for the seer to be right. If he or she is not one hundred percent accurate they are dismissed as charlatans and any knowledge they might have brought forth is largely ignored. It is the need to be right that distorts the accuracy of prophecy. And yet, who will listen to a seer who is wrong.

What an interesting dilemma.

There are any number of ordinary people having lucid dreams and receiving wakeful visions of the immediate events to come. This is happening more now than at any other time in history. But because the visions themselves are so grandiose these individuals are afraid to reveal their knowledge to others for fear of being labeled quirky. Who can blame them. Who in their right mind would want their picture plastered all over the grocery store tabloids headlined with whatever the publisher thought might sell his rags. Then there is the legitimate media to deal with. In our age of the "truth seeking, anything for a story" news coverage, clairvoyants and seers are quickly discredited whenever possible and put off to the shadowy side of society. This is so primarily because these individuals must be self-proclaimed. Afterall, there are no post secondary schools of study for metaphysicians. Not long ago every important family, yes even Christians, had an advisor who could look ahead to interpret the signs of immutable events. Some were very good, while others played at the art to make an easy living off the hopes and dreams of others. This still goes on.

Looking back to the good old days, what must John, the disciple of Jesus and writer of the Book of Revelation in the New Testament, have felt when writing down the images revealed to him of the end times. Clairvoyants, or visionaries know that individual images of distant future circumstances are not easily understood when experienced out of context to the whole vision of possibilities. John's experience was different in that he was given a series of images, strung together as an entire outline of what was to come. Imagine his complete awe at the visions: the image of the seven churches, angels, trumpets sounding from on high, the twenty-four elders seated around the throne of God, the scroll containing the seven seals, seven ghastly plagues, the great red dragon, the four horseman, the final battle of good over evil, the new vision of Jerusalem coming down out of heaven from God. The bigger question for John must have been how to interpret and record what he was being shown. The only way to insure that future generations would understand the deeper meaning of his final work was to encapsulate the visions in metaphor and symbolic language much the way he did later when incarnating as Michel de Nostredame in 1503.

The twelfth chapter of Revelation marks the turning point in John's vision, in that, chapters one through eleven describe what will happen before the Twelve Days of Light, and chapters thirteen through twenty-two give a very good account of what it will be like on earth after the Twelve Days for those who go unconscious.

It might have been emotionally easier for John knowing that two thousand years would pass before the manifestation of his visions. It seems hard to believe that the time of Revelation is, for all intent, now, a mere three years away. It seems hard to believe that we are the generation meant to experience the end of duality. It feels as though this revelation should still be for some distant, more fully aware generation. You know, individuals more willing to live outside the limitations of conflict. A generation of liberated beings comfortable with the true nature of consciousness as it relates to energy. But then, if it were to happen to a future generation, they too might feel as though more time was needed.

Then there are the accounts of the other John, who preaching in the desert declared, "The Kingdom of God is at hand." The prophet Isaiah, 800 years before John the Baptist's birth, spoke of his vision of a man in the distant future who would begin to prepare the collective mind for the revelation leading up to the final unification. Isaiah described John the Baptist as, *"The voice of one crying in the wilderness: Prepare the way of the Lord, make his path straight. Every valley shall be filled, and every mountain and hill shall be brought low, and the crooked shall be made straight, and the rough ways shall be made smooth; and all flesh shall see the salvation of God."* Luke 3: 4

The end of duality – when the rough is smooth the crooked made straight and <u>all</u>, with no exceptions, shall see the true nature of Creator God. For those who eventually go unconscious it will be just a two day glimpse.

ANCIENT RINGS OF LIGHT

"When the Spirit of truth comes, he will guide you into all the truth; for he will not speak on his own authority, but whatever he hears he will speak, and he will declare to you the things that are to come."
John 16: 13

We are constantly being bombarded by bands of energy emanating from the center of Creation. This has been the case since the very beginning. Within these nonphysical waves is the sustenance, the awareness enhancing unseen substance, often referred to as prana or chi that nourishes our Souls. We all know we need nutrients containing certain vitamins, minerals, carbohydrates, starches, fats, proteins and enzymes to sustain our physical vitality. We also need water, air and sunlight. Without these ingredients our physical vitality is lessened and if deprivation is prolonged, we disease and die. Our response to this energy wave could be compared to a plant being placed in sunlight. The presence of sunlight excites the plant to grow. The energy events emanating out from the center of Creation are our sunlight. Without these waves we would lapse into a deep unconscious slumber, unaware of ourselves or each other.

Mystics of all ages have tried to explain that we do not live by bread alone, but by an unseen food given to us from on high. This God fodder excites the dreams of what is possible within us (consciousness) and grants us the sustained focus to bring our imagining into manifest form (energy). Moses demonstrated this when he drew water from the stone and when, through the prayers of the elders, there was manna on the ground every morning for the Israelites to gather and eat as they journeyed toward the promised land.

For the most part, we can see the direct results these energetic cosmic waves have on individuals and the Collective Mind in the rise and fall of past civilizations. If we were to study the time intervals between and the duration of past civilizations, we would get a small and somewhat accurate glimpse of the pattern of energy constantly bombarding us from the center of Creation.

If we had the physical means to go back to the beginning of our Collective sojourn in this planetary system, we would also see that the greater waves of energy, one thousand years thick and 13,000 years apart, create alternating intervals of unification, then duality in the Collective Mind. This "grass is always greener" concept expressing at a cosmic level has us collectively pitching back and forth between external and internal validation, between separation and unification.

From the data we collect about past civilizations we may also conclude that not all waves are of the same quality, intensity or duration, and do not effect all individuals or groups of a certain time period in an equal fashion. Individuals respond according to their beliefs, therefore cultural influences play an important role as to the overall effect of the lesser waves of energy on individuals or circumstantial subsets within the Collective Mind. An example of this might be the difference between the Hindu belief that the physical human body is the major barrier to bliss and the Christian idea of the ascension of the physical body as demonstrated by Jesus. Buddhist or Hindu devotees might not understand why a Master teacher such as Jesus would teach the ascension of the physical body. After all, why take something that acts as a limitation in one dimension into what is perceived as the next higher reality?

The most common of these waves only measure hours thick and come one on top of the other in the same manner that waves meet the shore. These are the sustaining energy events we need to continue conscious awareness from moment to moment. Other waves are years thick and tend to create an age of activity, or a period of intellectual attitude. These bands of energy are constantly moving through our sector of space, and because they are of varying degrees, they have greater and lesser effects upon our external expressions of what is possible for ourselves individually and for the Collective Mind. In other words, the renaissance effect doesn't happen with all waves of energy.

13,000 YEAR INTERVALS

The Genesis story found in the Old Testament is a fragmented collection of symbolic images that attempts to relate the beginning of Creation and the happenings of thirteen thousand years ago. It was then that we moved from the unifying effect of the previous Lemurian wave 26,000 years ago into the polarized expression of separation that mythically marks the end of the Atlantis period thirteen thousand years ago. The last thirteen thousand years, from the breakup of Atlantis to the year 2001 is referred to in the Akasha as the Urantia epoch.

Again, each thirteen thousand year wave of energy is one thousand years thick by the time it overtakes our solar system. The effect at first goes relatively unnoticed by the masses with a few responding in profound realizations such as the sudden insights that led to the beginning of the renaissance. Toward the center of the wave everyone gets in on the act and a shift in the collective paradigm heralds the beginning of a new age.

Five hundred years ago the leading edge of such a wave began to excite our Collective Mind bringing us into a renaissance of body, mind and Spirit. Suddenly the earth was no longer flat and the center of the universe. In this age of technological triumph, the jump from a flat to a round world seems of no great consequence, but to the people of that period it was most disturbing and not very logical. Why hadn't the priest or scholars known about this all along? Imagine how those who were suppose to know felt. Their ability to comprehend creation was being challenged by a group of uninitiated merchants who suddenly knew they could circumnavigate the world. How absurd! The official word was being profoundly challenged. Those in power didn't seek their immediate execution for they were absolutely sure the foolhardy souls traveling west to find new routes to the east would find their demise and that would be the end of that. It wasn't until 1993 that the Catholic church officially agreed with the findings of Galileo. The church sent a letter to his descendants stating they were no longer excommunicated and could now enjoy the benefits of belonging to the one true faith.

Imagine how the thinkers of that time were inspired and frightened by this revelation of a round world. How did we keep from falling off into the stars? Newton explained our situation very clearly. In the present age gravity is a fundamental understanding. Then it wasn't. It was as though the minds of that time could miraculously look beyond the superstitions that governed their daily routines into an amazingly vast and suspiciously complex system of creation that defied their comprehension. To the great minds of that era there were no historical reasons to believe that anything special was about to happen. As a matter of fact, there was nothing, not even a prescience science fiction, to suggest that we would have the type of technological advancements that have been made since the middle 1400's. The truth is the vast majority of us are still governed by superstitious concepts eagerly fueled by our arrogance.

All that is about to change, as it did some five hundred years ago.

As is right for our time, scientists are genuinely baffled. But only because they have the means to be. Thank God we are no longer swayed by the church driven edict demanding ignorance for the masses that was in place during Galileo's time.

The following appeared in the Earth Watch section of the Atlanta Journal and Constitution newspaper on May 20th, 1995 and is attributed to staff reports and news services:

Puzzling Cosmic Rays

A mysterious force hurling particles at the earth with an energy so intense as to defy known physics, has brought scientists from around the world to Fermi National Accelerator Laboratory near Chicago to plot a counter attack. So far scientists have gotten good information on only two of the ultrahigh energy cosmic rays. Led by James Cronin, the University of Chicago's Nobel laureate physicist, cosmic ray researchers hope to assimilate a grid of ray detectors that would cover an area the size of Delaware.

The two known rays measured by scientists in Japan and Utah are charged with energies 100 million times greater than those produced at the Fermi Accelerator, which is the world's most powerful. Scientists say that even an explosion of the largest stars couldn't produce particles of such energy according to the laws of physics as they are now understood.

Ah, modern science. I find it interesting that Mr. Cronin is inspiring a counter attack. It would appear that science, in this age of great advancement, has assumed the role of the not so long ago church. This is the medieval mind set attempting to destroy something which is not easily, or immediately understood. What about reason, or at the very least, common sense. Wouldn't it be prudent, even to the most casual observer, to take a nonaggressive posture in a situation such as this. After all, if your enemy has a weapon 100 million times greater than anything you can come up with, isn't a counter attack somewhat futile? I would love to be there when they find out this energy is not physical in the terms that we understand with our laws of physics, and all they are able to measure is the effect this energy is having on the smallest of particles. It's like watching the wind blow through a field of grass. You can clearly see the effect of the wind, but not the wind itself. The Akasha measures the intensity at one hundred times that of our scientists – a hundred times a hundred million. The math is easy.

Again, this energy is nonphysical in nature. Yet, it is effecting physical matter indirectly through our redirection of this energy as amplified thought. Michael Talbot, in his book *"Holographic Universe,"* puts forth the idea that these subatomic levels of manifest form only came into existence at our insistence. They exist at our discretion. From the Akashic view point, Mr. Talbot is more right than he knows.

In the greater Knowing all that exists is consciousness and energy.

For the last thirteen thousand years, in our state of duality, we have expressed thought as <u>energy</u>. In a very short time we will have a complete understanding of the nature of reality and the relationship consciousness has with matter, and will once again express thought as <u>matter</u> as we did in the period from thirteen thousand to twenty six thousand years ago during the Atlantian and Lemurian epochs.

The lag time between our "science fiction" and its manifest reality is collapsing. As thought becomes matter, our desire for the mundane will suddenly vanish. We will no longer sit idly by hoping all turns out okay. We will be creating.

IN THE BEGINNING

"And God said, Let there be light; and there was light. And God saw that the light was good; and God separated the light from darkness. God called the light Day, and the darkness he called Night. And there was evening and there was morning, one day."
Genesis 1: 3-5

Most cultures, past and present, have at least one legend detailing the beginning of awareness in this realm. Some of the stories are wonderfully alive with rich details that satisfy our heart's connection to the planet and each other, such as those found in the telling of aboriginal peoples traditions. Others are couched in symbolic images that gratify the intellect's take on dimensional reality, as in those of modern Mideastern texts such as the Koran and Holy Bible. Whether of the heart or the intellect, neither explains much about our arrival here on the third rock from the sun. One thing we can all be sure of, the beginning happened a very long time ago.

The Akashic Records place our arrival here, in this solar system, some two hundred and six million years ago. Modern science, on the other hand, is convinced that intelligent life as we know it has existed for only the past twenty thousand years or so. That is tantamount to believing we are the only self-aware form of life in Creation, and that our solar system is the only such system in Creation. Science is now finding out that planets can exist without orbiting a star. In other words, we are changing our view of creation everyday.

We, the Collective Mind of the present duration, beginning thirteen thousand years ago, are the fifth such social experiment here upon the planet. Before us were Noh-Ah, Po-Seda, Lem-Ura (Lemuria), and At-Latia (Atlantis). Many individuals incarnating here now have their origins in the overlaping Lemurian and Atlantian periods.

Why then isn't there anything to be found of these ancient civilizations?

Many curious items from long before our modern time rest in

private collections and museums around the world. In the late 1800's and early 1900's collecting such curiosities was a popular hobby amongst the wealthy. Some of these collectors organized around certain beliefs and the modern science of archeology was formed. It was these individuals who decided there had to be an official version of our terra ferma progression. Unfortunately, if an artifact could not be explained within the forming opinions these individuals had of our past, it was dismissed and put to the side. A visit to the unexplainable items section of the Cairo Museum would reveal some of their less interesting discards. A look at the works of Erich von Daniken, replacing the UFO, gods from outer space spin, with notion of a technologically advanced culture of previous Earth inhabitants, would offer further disclosure of our heritage.

Now what of the obvious? Why haven't archeologists explained the pyramids or sphinx? No one has a definite explanation as to how and why, or who, for that matter. The science of archeology has fallen into the trap of only looking for evidence that supports its current perceptions of past reality. Look at how the prevailing view has recently changed concerning how dinosaurs lived. Once they were thought of as dull greenish gray, heartless, cold blooded reptiles. Now paleontologists describe them as colorful, warm blooded reptiles with very mammal like family qualities. Scientists. Go figure.

Then there is the matter of decay. If New York City were completely abandoned tomorrow, left to the elements, it would only take some four thousand years before only minute traces would be left. In five thousand years almost nothing would be left to indicate a city of its size was ever there. Look at how quickly and completely the structures of the Myan civilization were covered in a few hundred years. The point is, while science is good at observing and duplicating certain response patterns in energy and matter, it is completely inadequate as a means for investigating even the most recent distant past.

Genes versus Genesis: what of the creationist with their literal interpretation of the Bible? The Akashic Records show a similar version as is found in Genesis, Chapter One, but puts the date some two hundred million years earlier, and has the Garden of Eden on a different planet,

16

Maldec. Any references in Genesis to the placement of the Garden of Eden on Earth were later added. The Akasha shows that Maldec was an Earth sized planet orbiting Jupiter up until about six thousand to fourteen thousand years ago. This is a rather large window of time, mainly because of the difference in our and the Maldecian understanding of linear time. We might get a closer idea of when if we correlate its explosion to the freakish atmospheric and surface events of around eight thousand years ago. Take a look at *"Worlds in Collision,"* and *"Earth in Upheaval,"* by Immanuel Velikousky. Maldec's remains can be found in the asteroid belt between Jupiter and Mars, and Mars and Earth.

At this point in time all science has presented about our past is speculation and conjecture. That is why we remain confused as to how civilized man suddenly emerged on the scene some twenty thousand years ago. It is fortunate that locked within each of us is the memory of our beginnings here in this solar system. Without the cellular Knowing of our beginnings, we would have lost our vision of what was, is and is yet to be possible.

If the basic questions go unanswered by science and religion, when it comes to our presence on this little blue ball hanging in space, then what of the bigger questions? We know what feeds our physical bodies, but what feeds our Souls? How did human consciousness begin?

Science, in its silence, leaves these questions to mystics, who it then later seeks to disqualify because they do not follow the scientific model. Case in point: how did Albert Einstein know he was correct in his assumptions about energy as it appears in the form of light and matter? Why wasn't he talked out of his knowing when faced with such severe criticism from the learned elite? Read his autobiography. Einstein was a mystic. Mystics Know. Isn't it ironic that science now includes him as one of their own. Dilemma – we can navigate the solar system, orbit the moon of another planet millions of miles away and we are at a loss to explain how the Soul enters the physical body. We can split the atom or peer into galaxies far away, but have failed to discover why prayer has such a profound effect in healing.

For all the reasons we do, we continue to rely on this faulty concept called science to guide us forward. True, it has taken us out of the dark ages of the more dangerous superstitions, bringing us to the present time filled with intellectual insights as to the human predicament. What of the time ahead when we will all come from a greater Knowing, no longer needing proof to light our way. What about a future moment in which learning is displaced by Knowing? How can science allow Knowing? Will science try to stop the Collective moment of awakening that's just around the millennial corner by launching a counter attack against something it can not fathom? Will this be a modern Inquisition or the start of witch hunts by the religious right?

We know about mastery, but what of mystery? Can dissecting matter any further prepare us for the unknown awaiting us around each corner? Could it be that Michael Talbout was right about subatomic particles coming into existences as a response to our consideration of them? Is this an example of the new millennium where our thoughts create matter instantaneously? Could it be a mystical realization that the deeper we dive into the layers of matter, the more we are creating what we find. We will eventually discover that we are creating and rec-reating ourselves in each new moment while agreeing to a collective past.

What of the unseen beings living outside our sense's ability whose activity it is to aid us in fulfilling our dreams and visions of what is possible for ourselves and others? Has the blind faith of our current intellectually bound religions failed to address the true nature of the spirit realms? Who and what are the unseen agencies that guide and inspire us to greater Knowing?

Why are many individuals in mainstream America so willing to follow the edicts of self-proclaimed men of God who promise them eternal salvation for money?

Will science be able to explain what has happened to conscious-ness in the days immediately following our apex experience of this cur-rent thirteen thousand year energy event beginning in the year 2001?

To approach the answers to these questions we must look to the beginning. Beginnings are pregnant with the answers to questions asked at end times. These are the end times.

Genesis

The version of beginning most common here in the W[...] course the Abrahamic myth found in the Old Testament. This a[...] document contains a coded memory for the Collective Mind of wha[...] was like in the very beginning moments of dimensional reality, and the ensuing moment of separation. But before we begin the story of Genesis, it might be polite to offer an overview of the first book of the Old Testament, particularly for those unfamiliar with the text.

As an historical document it is clear that the early Mesopotamian culture heavily influences the first eleven chapters which trace the gradual expansion of humankind and the development of human culture. These chapters also illustrate the ambiguity of this development by incorporating stories about the sin of Adam and Eve and about the Deluge, both of which try to illustrate humankind's growing alienation from God and one another.

The universal outlook of the first eleven chapters gives way in chapter twelve as the focus narrows to one man and his family, Abraham. Yet the traditions about Abraham, Isaac, Jacob, and Jacob's twelve sons are linked to the earlier chapters by God's promise to bless the whole world through Abraham's descendants. Furthermore, the covenant established with Israel through the promise made to Abraham (Genesis 22: 15-18) is fundamentally the same as the covenant established with all of humankind through Noah (Genesis 9: 1-17).

Although Moses has traditionally been considered the author of Genesis, modern scholars generally agree that the book is a composite of at least three different literary strands: J (10th century BC), E (9th century), and P (5th century). One of the most difficult problems in interpreting Genesis has been distinguishing historical fact from the use of symbolic narration intended to convey a religious message. The controversy continues.

The Akasha views the beginning time a little differently and indicates chapter one of Genesis to be the vision, while chapter two is the manifest form of that vision. Chapter three is a description of the separation of unity into duality caused by the last great energy event, our previous Twelve Days of Light, at the height of the Atlantian culture.

In the Beginning

West is of
cient
it

veen the beginning moments described
ix days of the coming Twelve Days of
correlates with the seventh day of the
His Creation on the seventh just as an
ic Awareness on the seventh day of the
scious during the first six days.

the first three chapters of Genesis aloud,
Encoded in the text is a memory of the
last Twelve Days that is released into the surrounding etheric body of an
individual as the account is read aloud. It doesn't matter if you fully
understand or even agree with the message of Genesis. Reading it aloud
will work for everyone. The third chapter begs to be read with the understanding that it is describing duality, good versus evil in this case,
and our sudden awareness of it. For convenience sake, and for those
without Bibles, you will find chapters 1-3 in the notes section beginning on page 93.

An account of our Genesis from the Akasha:

1) The Being we refer to as God, was like us, in that, It incarnated
into dimensional realities to discover Itself, just as we have journeyed
here upon Earth and in other universe systems time and again. After
God had obtained to fullness through Its many encounters within the
limitations of Consciousness and Energy, and as Its final expression It
moved into the void, and, to use an analogy, turned itself inside out,
allowing every moment of all its many incarnational experiences to individuate into sentient and inanimate beings, such as ourselves and the
substance we call physical matter. We are, what is referred to in Genesis
1: 3, God's Light. Its images of Itself as It made Its way to Completion
through incarnation after incarnation. It is therefore, the manifest destiny of each Being (Us) to follow this same pattern and one day express
Ourself as the Source for all we have come to Know in our many encounter journeys through this vast Galaxy we call God. In other words,
each of Us will, at the end of our journeys, find ourself in the void and
a new universe within Galaxy God will be born in which each and every
one of our encounter moments will individuate as a new Being. We are

living in God as manifest forms of Its encounters, just as every one of our encounter moments will individuate into being, calling Us their Source for existing.

Imagine that each and every thought and feeling you experience in any one given day of this and all your lives is a seed for a Being to individuate into a complete form of life, just as an apple seed ultimately creates apples through the tree it becomes.

2) The firmament described in Genesis is the matrix, the medium, out of which all reality projects. The "waters" refers to dimensional reality as one reality expressing in many forms, such as water from ice to liquid to steam; the same basic form vibrating at different levels. This "in the midst" is also as Jesus had replied when asked, "Where is it you say you go?" "I go to prepare a place for you," and, "In my father's house there are many mansions."

Interestingly, the Akashic Records shows the physical dimension as the least real of all dimensional realities. The least real, meaning the least representative of the true nature of Creator God. But because this is where we encounter consciousness and energy it appears to be the most significant of all the other dimensions.

3) Each atom and molecule expresses an encounter of consciousness and energy that God had along Its way to completion. The base component for all matter is therefore the same. Everything at the level of Source is identical, i.e., water and dry land, the same. Animate, consciousness, and inanimate, energy, one and the same. To journey effectively to our end we have the many textures of that substance, the many places where consciousness and energy collide. The shore of the ocean is a metaphor for the separation of the base substance into distinctly different forms that caress and intermingle. The water at the shore is filled with sand, just as the sand at the shore is filled with water. It is hard to tell where God ends and we begin, just as it is hard to distinguish where we end and God begins. And yet we need a perceived separation to Know each other and God Creator.

We are one of the many forms of self-aware consciousness expressing in physical realms; and the physical worlds inhabited by others, like the waves against the shore, are too numerous to count.

4) The Akashic Records show a formula for one cell of consciousness whether it is mineral, plant or animal. It also shows only one form of energy. The atoms that form our bodies and ultimately allow us to have a sensate experience of this realm are God Creator expressing in Its greatest simplicity.

The genetic line of each physical form, whether mineral, plant or animal, is the evolutionary paper trail, so to speak, back to its Source, the One Substance.

We, all of Us, are evolving to our own unique Fullness. This also suggests our destiny in that seeds bear their same kind. We are in God's image. Our journey, as God's journey, is the same - to journey to Fullness as God has done before us, giving birth to the many encounter seeds within us.

5) As consciousness joins with energy, the resonating octaves that are generated create cycles of light which form matter. Later, the concept of cycles became our consideration of time.

The Akasha shows the beginning of this realm in two forms, micro and macro. Micro in the sense that you can look back over the moment of Creation from the perception that it has a beginning and an end, and therefore took a period of time. Macro in that Creation is still in the moment of itself.

The perception of time, in and of itself, is a problem. Time is wholly arrogant in that it presupposes a vantage point as dimensionally fixed; and yet there is no other term suitable to the intellect to express a duration of event other than time. Moments are big, beyond time; beyond our comprehension. The macro expression of reality is one eternal moment, beyond the limits of time. However, we, as the conscious consideration of reality, need a measure. Time seems to be it for now. And, just like the earth was once flat to our perception, time, in the very near future, will cease to be linear and only a consideration of the intellect. We will go back to the use of cycles. Nostradamus used planetary cycles and alignments as a way of placing a future event in a fixed time. Not completely successful, but wonderfully sound in consideration.

6) As far as God being off in another place, the Akashic Records show that we have had help from several races of beings not native to

this world through the genetic re engineering of our DNA and nervous systems. We are just now coming to understand how this is possible through our experiments with cloning.

These visitors helped to further insure our quickened evolution by implanting memories of worlds beyond our everyday circumstances so that we might have a future memory, a vision of where we were going. They have come three times, each time changing the human genetic blueprint to allow us greater awareness of ourselves as consciousness and energy. It is impossible to place these alterations exactly in linear time, primarily because these events happened when the concept of time was substantially different than it is now. In other human activity events that pre date the concept of time, there are references to correlating events. Regarding our alien friends, there are no sequence markers in the Records to indicate a linear placement in the events of human consciousness. This is so with many of their encounters with us. It is as though these encounters happen out of time in our way of thinking.

The Akashic Records indicate the root race of all humans to be Black. After several genetic alterations orchestrated by our space friends from the Pleiades, and Orion, the Oriental race emerged from the Black. This "new" race eventually formed the civilization of Lemuria that existed approximately 52,000-20,000 BCE.

The majority race in Atlantis (20,000-13,000 BCE) was a beautiful mixture of the root race and the "new" genetic strain – Black and Oriental. After the break up of the Atlantian civilization thirteen thousand years ago, the survivors split into two groups. One of the groups joined with the Lemurian remnant that had moved up through Mexico and formed what we think of as the Red race. With a little more genetic engineering from our space friends, the Black and Oriental mixture of Atlantis eventually became the Caucasian race that emerged in the Middle East in the Tigris and Euphrates River valleys. Around 10,000 BC the Caucasian race began mixing with the remnant of Atlantis. This mixture gave us the blood lines now prevalent in the Mid East. To further complicate the genetics of the Caucasians, the Oriental Tibetans moved into Europe and mixed with the Caucasians to form the Slavic bloodlines of Northern Europe and Russia. It is important to note that there have also been human forms that were allowed to naturally select and evolve. The aliens wanted a pure strain to compare against their achievements.

The Akashic Records show that the pure bloodlines are now dying out in favor of the mixed genetics of the "new" races engineered with the help of aliens. This new race, a genetic blend of all the races, will be better able to withstand the coming energy changes that are about to take place on the planet. The Records also show this combined race will be the new root race for the next great civilization to inhabit Earth. The previous race was of this planet. The new race will be star seed.

Also, it was through their interference that we eventually gained dominion over the other animal forms. This was to insure that the number of human beings on the planet would be sufficient to create a collective mind large enough to make this final shift to fifth dimensional awareness.

It is extremely important to Know that all was set into motion from the beginning vision, and that God Knows Itself through all its evolving forms of expression. There is no judgement as to higher or lower forms of life. This is the simplicity of God. Dominion means that we are to be as Creator to this world, giving life anew in each moment, just as it has been given to us.

7) The apex of the present thirteen thousand year energy event from the center of Creation is of course the six and seventh days of the twelve consecutive days. The first six days will be filled with a new sense of wonderment at the reality of nature which will lead the fully conscious individual into a profound Creation stage of awareness that culminates in the final transmutation of the DNA of the physical body beginning on the fifth day and lasting through the end of the seventh day. This transmutation is our jump from separation into Unity and allows consciousness and energy an unlimited dance within Creation. This is shown in the Records as a day of complete rest, where body, mind and Spirit become as One.

A look from both sides. The micro view of unfolding grace: on the sixth day every moment of every encounter that Creator had ever experienced was released to find Its Way to Fullness. This full circle from

24

beginning to beginning. This is our destiny foretold to us by the One who Created our existence.

From the macro view – nothing need be added to that which is Created. All is Known. It ended in the moment it began.

Other Beginning Accounts

The first three chapters of the First Book of Moses were an attempt to record the orally preserved account of an event that had happened some six thousand years prior to the initial writing of Genesis. The only other ancient source of information about this event is found in the two dialogues of Plato – *Timaeus* and the *Critias*. Plato recounts in the *Timaeus* that Egyptian priests, two hundred years before Plato's birth, had described Atlantis as a powerful empire seeking to dominate the Mediterranean world eleven thousand five hundred years ago. In this account the expansionist plans of the Atlantans ended only when they were defeated by the Athenians. Shortly after their defeat an earthquake shattered the island of Atlantis, splitting it in two, causing it to sink beneath the ocean. The Records show this legend to be a metaphor used to describe the last thirteen thousand year event. In the *Critias*, Plato characterizes the Atlantian as possessing an ideal culture filled with technological wonders beyond those of other nations. The nature of its utopian political system has been discussed extensively by many later writers. Interestingly, some of those writers speculated that the present-day American Indians migrated from the Old World to the New by way of Atlantis. When the two chambers existing on either side of the King's chamber in the great pyramid attributed to Cheops are opened we will have records of the genetic experiments and later migrations of the Lemurians and Atlantans. We will no longer have to speculate.

Atlantis Revisited – Prior to their Twelve Days

Their culture was different from ours in that they had developed the sun as an energy source for their industries and used thought energy, redirected through silica based amplification devices, to power everything from air conditioning to elevators to personal transporta-

25

tion devises.

Conflict of any kind was unknown to the Lemurians and Atlantian. Stress and disease, therefore, was also unknown. That is why they were able to use streams of thought energy as the basis of their power. Medicine was not an integral part of their culture until about twenty five years before the transition to duality. The beginning presence of duality began creating distress in the most sensitive and aware individuals, often those leading the culture. It was their demise that left the Atlantans without a vision to guide them into the mysterious realms of duality- right and wrong, good versus evil.

Other unknowns prior to the transition include: gender bias, greed, hunger, manipulation, power and war. Those held in high regard were individuals who could express the simplest, most direct answer to any question. These were often individuals who had devoted their lives to service. Mother Theresa would be one such individual.

Due to the telepathic and teleportive nature of their society, ownership was universal. There was nothing to hide, no walls or fences. No laws or courts. Imagine, no petty officials. Prisons would seem barbaric to these non-judgmental beings. There were guardians, individuals who held the vision of unification, to guide and direct the general activities of the collective mind. Their understanding of Creator was limitless sound, color and form. Individual creative expression was regarded as a sacred manifestation of the collective mind appearing through one being.

After their Twelve Days

The culture of Atlantis experienced the energy event of thirteen thousand years ago as the beginning of duality, the expulsion from the Garden of Eden as described in Genesis. Prior to this all consciousness expressed as one. The highly sensitive within the collective mind began to feel the effects of the wave and started the process of separation some five hundred years before the apex at the center of the wave, just as has happened at this time. These sensitive individuals were the "Eve" factor who tempted others to awaken to this new powerful force of duality.

In chapter three of Genesis we first encounter duality as Eve is beguiled by the serpent. The serpent symbolically represents the subtle vertical Earth energies that became realized as the energy of the thirteen thousand year event began to expand individual awareness. We presently know this vertical force as the kundalini resting at the base of the spinal column. As we approach our present Twelve Days we will once again become profoundly aware of this force in nature as our awareness expands in response to the current thirteen thousand year wave.

At the apex of the energy event human consciousness in Atlantis became two equal forces, one of feminine polarity that included all physical matter, the other as a masculine polarity that encompassed all etheric manifestation. Two great gatherings of souls began to take form within the collective – those who followed the Law of One (feminine) and those who followed Belial (masculine). It needs to be noted that the definition of masculine and feminine was not based on gender; individuals were defined by their attributes. Gender was simply a reproductive function and had nothing to do with the definition of an individual's being. Prior to this energy event all reproduction was guided from the etheric realms by the soul wishing to take a physical form, not by the unbridled lust for physical gratification, not that there was anything wrong with a little unbridledness back then.

The Law of One gathering moved out into nature finding balance in the cycles of Earth as they occupied what we now think of as the American hemispheres and surrounding islands. A small band went into Europe via England and established what we think of as the Druids. The great stone circles and mounds of western Europe, such as Stonehenge and the serpent mounds of North America are the altars at which they prayed.

The followers of Belial continued technology as their outward expression, building great monuments to their ideas of God/Creator. The early Mediterranean cultures were created by Belial, an actual individual who later took the name, Thoth, as he inspired the creation of the Egyptian culture. The pyramids and sphinx at Giza were his creation and are the only surviving relics from the Atlantian culture. The Atlantian had no need for the written word, so documentation of the pyramids' origins could be left to the future whims of those grappling for power.

The gods of early mythology are those individuals who remained fully conscious during the last Twelve Days of Light and decided to stay with the planet as it moved into the next thirteen thousand year cycle. They acted as custodians of knowledge, passing along truths in story form to inspire human consciousness to conduct itself according to what they believed were universal laws. A portion of this is recounted in the story of Moses as he received the Commandments from God on Mount Sinai. Moses was one of those who remained unified after the Atlantian Twelve Days, incarnating in human form at the ascribed time to co-lead the Hebrews through the wilderness toward the promise land with Mirium. The journey of the Hebrews, from the 10th century BC to now, has been a micro view of the sojourn of human consciousness upon the Earth.

Our New Beginning – A little shaky at first
We enter this time of renewal with very little more to go on than those who witnessed this same sort of transition thirteen thousand years ago. The great minds of science, with their need to be right, and the heads of religion, with their need to instill blind faith as a condition for entering heaven, have blinded mainstream individuals and themselves to the events of the coming days. The shift to fifth-dimensional awareness is not going to be easy for most people. The struggle that moving from duality to unification brings to multitudes is not unlike the trauma Adam and Eve felt when being cast out of the circumstances they were familiar with. If change is difficult for the average human, imagine what it is for the entire collective mind.

Those who continue to seek power after the Twelve Days will invite all manner of sorrow upon human consciousness. The good news: the final conflict of duality that expresses over the twenty-five years from 2001 - 2026 will melt into a thousand years of peace and joy.

RESPONSE SCENARIOS

"Lo, I am coming like a thief! Blessed is he who is awake..."
Revelation 16: 15

At some moment in the middle of the year 2001 we will find ourselves at the apex point of the present thirteen thousand year energy event. Everyone will experience this phenomenon at the same time and much in the same manner, at least as far as the initial energy display is concerned. After that each individual's approach to life will begin to show in exaggerated ways.

There is little an individual can do to insure a smooth transition into the New Age. It doesn't matter if you've spent the last twenty years in complete denial of your spiritual nature or lived each of the tenants of your core beliefs to their fullest. You will experience the revelation of how consciousness plays out its adventure with energy during those first few days of the Twelve. The actual circumstances of how the Twelve Days unfold will be determined by your willingness to let go of past conflicts and future anxieties. In other words, there is nothing special you need do to prepare for this event; your many incarnations since the last wave, during the time of Atlantis, have been the preparation. You have all the abilities needed to remain fully conscious for the duration. What is important is the understanding that judgment and conflict are what have always kept you from a full experience of life. This will become very apparent during the first Three days of the Twelve.

There are any number of scenarios that will play out in the first two days. The three different response patterns of individual revelation presented here are the extreme case scenarios in each of the three distinctly different levels of experience shown in the Akasha. Those levels could be described as:

1 – Self validating inspired creator
2 – Savior validated permission seeker
3 – Punishment cleansing blame placer

Again, these are in no way the only response patterns available

29

during the first three days. Individuals within a particular culture will have general tendencies peculiar to that group based on the evolving belief systems of that group. These scenarios are generalizations of the levels, not cultural norms. Each level of response will include all the elements of the others to varying degrees. The willingness to move into the next level of perception is what determines the overall experience of the Twelve Days.

The First Two Days – Scenario #1

You are standing in the kitchen about seven fifteen in the morning after a very restful night's sleep. You thumb through your most recent purchase, *The Tibetan Book of Living and Dying*, by Sogyal Rinpoche, while waiting for the coffee maker to finishing brewing a very special Sumatran Gold blend you found at the local brew house. Ah. First sip. Warm roasted flavors fill your mouth to overflowing. It's the beginning of what promises to be yet another wonderful summer day.

Without warning, the Proctor Silex toaster, the new one that cooks your favorite bagels to a perfect golden hue, seems not only to be glowing from the inside, but somehow is glowing from the outside as well. You rest your coffee cup on the counter and bend closer to check it out.

The white outer coating is glowing a soft greenish blue. The cord is giving off a beautiful indigo halo, and where it disappears into the electrical socket is a magnificent purple. A delightful tingle runs up your fingers as you run your hand across its surface. All the sockets appear the same as you look around the room. The cords leading to the unused appliances have less glow. You step back, rub your eyes, and put on glasses to get a better view.

The herb garden in the greenhouse window behind the sink is a rainbow of energetic color. The terra cotta pots broadcast a brilliant red against the lavender and pink hues of the plants. There are wisps of energy moving around and through the flowering plants as though an etheric butterfly is fluttering from bud to bud. You smile at knowing the glowing movement is a deva spirit.

Everything in the room is emanating varying degrees of soft glowing light. With very deliberate motions, so as not to disturb anything, you move to the phone to call your spiritual mentor. Through it all this individual has not only been an outstanding teacher, but dear friend. This is the one person in the world you can tell everything to without hesitation.

You soon discover you're both having the same experience. All the metaphysical classes the two of you attended over the last fifteen years talked to the subject of consciousness and energy, but before today you had never seen an aura, not even a hint. You agree to begin calling family and friends to see if this is happening to everyone. You also agree to stay indoors and to check on each other by phone every evening until this passes.

The task of talking to someone who's not of like mind, who's confused and frightened by the events of the morning, proves exhausting. Some friends and family members are panicking, not sure if they're going crazy, or if it's just a recreational drug flash back from the sixties, while others tell you to call back because they can't talk now. You intuitively know it's because they're trying to get through to their minister or spiritual advisor, and can't. A deep compassion for their apparent confusion and spiritual suffering sweeps over your heart. Soft rings of pinkish gold light spread out toward them from your heart chakra.

As the day goes on you notice that, not only does everything have a particular halo effect, but it also has a distinct sound that has obviously been out of true hearing range all this time. Suddenly you realize you can't imagine how it was that you related to your world prior to this morning. How dull it must have been.

Everything is becoming crystal clear – your thoughts are focused in such a way as to immediately bring each question to conclusion. As a matter of fact, it's as though your mind immediately knows both the question and the answer. There's no lag time, no gap.

You note in your journal, "At the end of the first day all substance is giving off energy, light, in equal measures. At first only electrical appliance, those things needing generated power were glowing. The greater the use of power the greater the glow. Space seems more blue; earth is yellow. The fire of the candle is a spectacular red while the water in the offering dish is not as clear as it is white. All substance is breathtakingly

31

beautiful. The rock on the window sill and the delicately crafted vase in the foyer are equally impressive. All plants have a similar hue spectrum, with the larger plants showing layers of intensity in their auras. The cat seems unbothered by all the revelation, as though nothing special is happening. Perhaps this is normal for her. The most exciting part of her presence is the gentle orange halo produced by her purr. Interestingly, it is accompanied by a earthy musty odor."

The light in front of you, and particularly above you, begins to become thicker as you read your notes out loud. You try singing. High notes bring a foggy like appearance to the energy. Low notes have less effect. The more rapid the succession of notes, the more lasting the effect. High rapid utterances create a shimmering like substance out of the light. You try the names of God learned in Kabbhalah classes. In-credible swirls and spirals spin out from your mouth, filling the room with thick radiant light.

Next you try the mantra you've been practicing in group all week. You begin, "OM BENZA SATTO HUNG," take a deep inhalation and continue, OM VAJRA SATTVA HUM," while envisioning all who have gone before you to be purified of all karma. Thousands of rays of light in every color imaginable stream out from your head and heart joining the light already present in the room.

"Magnificent!" you exclaim in wonder. The chakras at the center of your body are a brilliant array of energy. "Magnificent!"

Your friend answers the phone before it rings. You both agree that even though you are miles away, it's as if you were standing there hug-ging one another. It's very different using the phone knowing its sur-face boundary isn't what it seems. As a mater of fact, you haven't wanted to use electrical devises at all. They seem to interfere with the light emanating from your own body. You know electricity isn't harmful to you, it just seems to dull the overall color of your etheric body.

What a day!

Out of habit you begin preparing for bed. "Is everyone seeing their bodies like this?" you say aloud staring into the mirror at what normally is your nude physical form.

Layers of light cover you from head to toe, wrapping you in a warm terry cloth sensation. The outermost layers are strong brilliant hues, while the inner colors over the seven central chakra centers are softer and more subtle in their display. You watch for what seems an eternity. The water feels so comforting as it spills and splashes its way toward the drain. The presence of humidity shimmers the colors radiating from your body, blending them into a gelatin looking field of hues all contained within an energetic envelope surrounding your body. The soap adds another quality to the magnificent array. Images of you and your lover crowd the space around you. You wonder what making love will feel like, sound like, look like.

The delicious sensations of towels, pajamas, and sheets all become distractions to your habitual desire to sleep. After all, you muse, with all that has happened you should be tired. Sleep never comes. As soon as you thought to go to bed, you were refreshed. All day long that's been happening – you noticed it was time to eat, but then felt full. Thirst quenched itself. There has been no gap in your experience all day long. Only fullness and wholeness. The night passes quickly. Sleep was replaced by a deep conscious rest filled with dreamlike sequences of thought, energy and form. It's as though every thought flashes sparkles of light around the periphery of your mind. Within the center of all this activity is a calm eye-of-the-storm knowing. Peace beyond mind.

The alarm chimes seven, the same time you awoke yesterday.

"The day and the night being the first full day," you say aloud.

As you lay there wondering what could possibly be next, you remember how wonderful it is to play with dreams, that you love to wake up a little early in the morning just to consciously drift off into feelings and images. Lucid colors begin to form in familiar shapes of past and possible feelings carrying you into magnificent dreamscapes. Every thought presents itself in geometric patterns as you create realities from light, moving your awareness at will between holographic layers of parallel dimensions.

In the next moment the sun is breaking through the window. The energy events of yesterday are shining even greater today. Light is everywhere. Sparkles of energy crowd your sight as each thought attempts to manifest instantly before your eyes. It's as though the thoughts themselves are trying to manifest as reality. Time collapses into Creativity. The day is effortless.

You try to remember the you of two days ago. Old feelings of not belonging to the death obsessed world culture grip at your body, cramping your abdominal muscles, sending you running to regurgitate years of judgment against your fellow man. Sickness moves through every cell of your body as you release all feelings of conflict, guilt and shame. Self judgment slips away leaving only a vague memory of hurt feelings, misunderstanding and expressions of anger. Your body feels clean. New. Infant. No shadows of doubt or fear. No resentments squeezing the life out of each molecule. That reality seems unable to attract your attention or contain your awareness. You can't imagine ever having had those considerations. That reality seems like a very far distant dream. A different world from this world of light and joy.

You look at the clock, it's already evening. The entire day has been spent just like yesterday indoors – to yourself in your womb, creating in images shaped by feelings constructed out of light. You are truly creating for the first time in your life. Not concerned about anything but the extreme joy of Creating. It's like nothing you've ever known. And it is so familiar, so right.

It's seven PM. The evening meal, a time you used to reflect on daytime achievements, seems unimportant. It's as though the activities of the day fed your hunger. You remember your friend and call. In that exact moment they're calling you. You have had identical days, finding joy in all your discoveries. No longer concerned for resources or outcome. Joy in the moment of joy.

Again you rest out of the habit of resting. It seems oddly important to honor the cycles of the sun even though the light emanating from everywhere and everything has eclipsed its rays. Now there is only light, a powerful radiance, friendly to your eyes. Conscious sleep comes as your physical body purrs in rest. You are completely conscious of every moment while you rest. No unconscious desire can be found within you. The thought of an unconscious reality strikes you as absurd. Thought and feeling are one. You now are moving in mystical realms where thought no longer expresses as energy. Thought is now substance.

34

The day and the night, the second day.

Seven chimes bring your awareness fully back into your body. To-day, the third day, you fully realize that each thought you entertain becomes reality. No longer are thoughts just sparkles of light dancing in the periphery of your vision. You immediately invite the presence of all the great souls that have gone before you. Luminous spheres of light form out of the deep blue of space as the presence of those beings who held the light of compassionate love begin to guide and direct your awareness as it moves into the great mystery beyond time. Your soul soars as your conscious mind becomes one with theirs. Thunderous claps astound your awareness as Jesus, Quan Yin, Buddha and numer-ous others gather to welcome you. Their limitless generosities of being send waves of gratitude that lift your body, mind and Spirit to ecstasy. You know you will always be.

The First Two Days – Scenario #2

You are standing in the kitchen about seven fifteen in the morning after a troubled night of caring for your mother's recent bout with a chronic respiratory infection. She's finally resting.

"It has been very difficult for her since father died," you remind yourself aloud as you gather breakfast things to the counter. "It was hard on all of us." You notice you forgot and left the butter out all night. It's partially melted. You shrug heavy shoulders and continue.

"She's hardly said a word since he died. What's she waiting for? Why can't she get on with her life," you ask out loud as you thumb through the food section of the paper looking for bargains. The coffee maker gurgles and sputters as the last drops of the generic blend you found at the Price Club makes its way into the pot. You're surprised at the first sip. It immediately tastes better than the brand your sister gets at the specialty store. You're glad at the triumph. Finally something to brag about. With that spark of joy, the day suddenly promises to be a good one.

You turn to get the sweet rolls from the pantry and notice a strange light shimmering around the stuffed shelves of the small storage space. You switch the pantry light off, but the pantry keeps shimmering. Without closing the door you back into the center of the room. Your hand makes it to your wide open mouth as you draw in a deep breath.

"Dear God! It...They...I'm...Dear Lord!" is all you can manage at the sight. You spin around then steady yourself against the counter top. Everything is glowing in the same shimmering light. Soft effervescent streams of light are pouring at you from all directions. You reach out a hand to touch the glowing surface of the refrigerator. It touches you back. Childlike joy fills your body. Then fear. Now self doubt. You look around to see if anyone is watching. You touch again. It touches back.

"God have mercy!" Your mind races back to the Sunday School class you attended just last week. The visiting youth minister had talked about the coming days and the signs that would soon show themselves to those who had accepted Jesus as their personal Lord and Savior.

The trip down the hall takes only a second. "Mother, wake up! This is what they've been telling us about. I'm sure of it. Look," you say, sweeping a hand though the air. Trails of energy follow the movement of your body. A deep feeling of anticipation fills the room as your mother slowly awakens.

Her tired body groans as she pushes upward on the pillows, eyes half closed in weakness. A rattle punctuates her weary sigh.

"Mother!" she suddenly exclaims, eyes wide, looking past you to the center of the room.

Over your shoulder a luminous cloud of shimmering light is gathering above the table against the wall. Tears fill your eyes as the features of your grandmother come into view.

"What took you so long, Mother. I've been waiting here for the longest time. Who's that with you, Uncle Jack?" your mother asks as she sits forward away from her much needed support. A beautiful greenish blue gathering of light quickly appears at your grandmother's side.

"No, dear child, it's Thomas come to get you." The comforting voice of your grandmother, the voice that had sung you to sleep so many times rings softly inside your head. The gathering light at her side takes a human like form.

"Father?" Sudden overwhelming confusion fills your mind as you step toward the end of the bed.

A sweet honeysuckle smell fills the air as your grandmother's voice becomes your father's. "Dear lady, may I have this dance?" You had heard him say it to her a million times. It was one of your fondest memories to watch him bow as he asked her. Then lifting her from the dinner table chair, he would glide her across the room.

Your mother sits up in a burst of energy, folds her legs under her and stands on her knees in the middle of the bed. "I was so mad at you for leaving me behind. Mother, tell him. Tell him how angry I've been. A body shouldn't be so lost." Your mother's voice is young, excited.

Both light forms reach out to hold her hands. The shimmering light coming from your mother's weak body fills the room to overflowing as she stands to take their hands.

"Mother, you mustn't stand on..." you scold, reaching out to stop her from hurting herself. The light coming from her shifts to a deep pinkish purple. Her physical body drops back to the bed as her soul steps forward to join those who have come to relieve her aloneness. Young and full of life she's standing next to your father again. Just as she used to.

A flash of light blinds you and without warning everything in the room has shifted. Grandmother is gone. Your mother and father are standing before you at an altar. She speaks softly into your heart.

"It is the time they spoke of. This is the revelation. You are witness to the coming of the Holy Spirit upon mankind. Rejoice, for this is the day of our Lord. He is to be with you this day."

All the years of wondering if you were enough; good enough, giving enough, doing enough. Belonging to get approval. Approval to feel good about yourself. All the years of wanting to please to get permission wail up inside, making it hard to hear her words. Waves of distress shake your body. Panic.

"What have I done with my life?" you ask sitting on the end of the bed next to the discarded body, ignoring those standing in front of you. You feel stunned. Disoriented. "The bed's a mess. Gotta make the bed." You hurry, then stop. An urgent question is forming like a bubble deep inside your head. It quickly breaks the surface of your conscious mind.

"What was the point of all this? Why was I ever born," you ask yourself as you struggle to pull your mother's body right in the bed. You straighten the bed clothes, placing her pillow just as she likes it. Her final resting place. You smile at her unmoving expression.

The remainder of the day goes by in what seems like an eternity of self examination as you check and balance your years upon earth, looking at each and every detail, making sure of your intention, putting right those things left undone. It's as though you can't stop, you mustn't stop this process.

The visions of your life begin to make sense. Your sister always thinking you the favorite. Your children never fully appreciating your sacrifice. Your former husband betraying your devotion. All were there to test your inner strength. To forgive, that was the point. To see the correctness in every word and deed. Just as He would have done. No blame. No guilt.

"Turn the other cheek. If someone steals your coat, give them your cloak. Love your enemies. Love each other as I have loved you." A calm permeates the moment. "It was a test! Life is a test of perseverance," you conclude in a loud powerful voice.

Flashes of past moments bounce against each other in a mindless array. Visions of all the turning points that have guided you here to this moment are so immediately real as you continue the examination. A sense of purpose replaces the endless depression of the last few years. It's at the same time exhilarating and exhausting as conflict after conflict is resolved.

Revelation fills you from the inside out. "I have been a good person," you declare. Light streams out of your mouth, filling the room around you with a heavenly glow.

"I have always acted out of interest in the needs of others. I have put others first to insure harmony. I was taught by good people to fear the Lord and to keep the Commandments." A constant out pouring of golden energy from your face and chest adds luster to hues of color already spilling around the room.

"I did my very best to keep my word to others. It was my bond of trust that never failed me. And I truly forgave others when they couldn't honor their word, or follow as closely to the Word of God as I did. I gave a good example." The glow suddenly shifts into a misty light. Self judgement grabs at your mid body cramping tissue, doubling you over in pain. A wave of tired feelings sinks you to the bed. Unconscious sleep overtakes you. Rest. So much has happened in so short a time. Your whole life. So short. So little time. Unconscious rest. Dreams. Troubled. Joyful. Dreams within dreams.

Then as if kissed by an angel you awaken. The light is brighter if that's possible. Immediately you go to check on your mother, then remember the day before.

"No wait! What day is it?" You remember the clock in the phone has the day displayed along with the time. Eight-thirty AM on the 18th.

This being one day and night.

It seems like days and days have gone by since this all began. "I'll call about mother's body. Reverend Williams will know what to do. He was so good with father."

The phone rings repeatedly, then just as you are about to hang up, the reverend answers in a very tired voice. His hello is weak. He seems so scattered in his thoughts and feeling. You are instantly amazed at how much you know about him. You've never had a feeling like this before. You know his mind completely. You feel his heart. Everything is crystal clear about this man who has long guided your spiritual life. In all the years you never knew this much. He's pulling at you, hoping you have something to quiet the confusion.

Your voice feels clear and strong as you answer his unspoken question. "Reverend, you know this is the rapture don't you. It's His time come. This is the time you've spoken of so often lately. It's the Holy Spirit, the Comforter." You feel a shiver run through him. "It's the baptism by fire."

"How can you be so sure?" His normally soft assuring voice is edged with distrust and anger. "All the calls. People not understanding my words." A pleading texture of motherly feelings tug at your heart as he continues. "She's gone. Left. My wife left. Can't find her anywhere. I've looked all over the house. She was here, then gone in the middle of all this light. You were friends. Has she called you?" He pauses. "Hello,

hello."

What to say. Nothing would do. "Good bye, Reverend." You gently place the phone in its cradle, not wanting to disturb his pleading thoughts.

There's nothing left to do. It's done. You stare into the wall above the table where your mother joined your father. Joy for her, sorrow at your aloneness. Tears fill your eyes wishing you too could have gone.

Another flash of light takes your sight.

"Let go your burden. Lift up your heart unto Me. This is my promise fulfilled. Today you will be with me, at my side."

A beautiful figure stands at the alter where your father and mother had disappeared. Rainbows of color are emanating out from every pore of his being.

"It is Him!" you shout, looking around for confirmation. There is only you here in this moment with Him. Thrilled feelings swell up inside. He with you. You don't have to share. A nervous giggle breaks the seal of your lips.

"It's You!" Joy fills you beyond compare. Not a doubt exists in your mind. It's Him. "This is the rapture, isn't it? You're here for the faithful. Do I need to...?...I mean who takes care of all...?" Child like joy fills every pore of your body. You feel as though you've come home. "I love that song, "In The Garden." It fills me every time I sing it. I knew the first time I heard it as a child that I'd be with you again. Thank you for holding my hand all these years. I so needed you. Can I be in heaven? Am I good enough?"

"By your faith you come unto Me," Jesus instructs in a joyous burst of sound. "By your faith."

In that instant your physical body radiates a brilliant golden glow. You look back and the same is happening to your mother's discarded form. You're both raising up off the bed, upward toward Jesus. All your life you've dreamed of this, from the time you were a little girl. You look back expecting to see both your physical bodies dead on the bed. They're not. They...you've been transfigured, like Jesus on the mountain top.

The earth is far behind you. A distant memory as you continue upward. A sound so beautiful fills your ears. It's like all the choirs you've

40

ever heard, all singing together in joyous celebration. Out of the light emerge images of wings and soft flowing gowns. Hundreds. No thousands. Legions of Angels all spiraling upward in a great arch toward a magnificent star. You are one. The power of your wings delights your sense of knowing. You thrust upwards to join others who have been of service. The higher you climb away from the Earth, the more expanded you become. You have room for so much. And there is a peace. Peace outside mind. Joy everlasting. Eternal rest unburdened from the life long struggle of trying to be enough.

The First Few Days – Scenario #3

You are standing in the kitchen at about seven fifteen in the morning trying to shake off the previous night of cards, cigarettes and beer. You push through the clutter on the sink counter. The TV headlines coming at you from the other room are declaring the previous day's toll on humanity. Day old coffee boils over in the microwave. Damn! Too hot. The bitter acid wash of coffee chases away the kerosene odor of your morning breath.

It's the beginning of what promises to be yet another day in paradise.

"Yeah, right," you mutter as you throw the scrawny cat off the counter and onto the floor. It hisses a protest your way, then runs for the pet door to take refuge outside.

The toaster seems to be reflecting light from somewhere in the room. You move across the counter away from the distraction. The glow seems even stronger where you are now standing.

"Hmm." You spin around as if you could check every direction simultaneously.

"Where's it coming from," you say aloud, immediately annoyed at the mystery.

You look over to get the jar of grape jelly and suddenly realize that the light reflecting off the toaster is somehow bouncing all over the room. Everything is glowing.

"What the Sam Hell...," you sputter. "Honey," you shout toward the back of the house.

41

As you round the corner, she's backing down the hall toward you acting as though she's just seen a ghost. The radiant glow surrounding her body moves away from her in layers of red, orange and yellow. You look down and discover you are suffering the same affliction.

"My god," she cries out, "What's happening to us?"

"I don't know, Baby." Suddenly you like the way she's clutching at you. It feels like old times. A rush of sexual sensations tightens the muscles in your lower belly. "Sit here while I'll get the number for the preacher man." You fumble your way through the Yellow Pages, not wanting to touch the glowing mass of ads. The touch tones of the phone tickle deep inside your head as you impatiently punch the dial pad. It's busy. You hit the redial. At seven rings you quit counting.

"No one's there," you announce with disgust. "The one time you need that smooth talking son-of-a-bitch and he's nowhere to be found. I'll call the kids and see if it's the same at their place."

"What is it, John? What's it doing?" Your wife's body is completely engulfed in a brilliant red glow. She's holding out her arms, examining her hands. "Am I dreaming, John?" Her eyes pleading for an answer. "It's red, but it's not hot. Why am I doing this."

"Hell, I don't know. Maybe it's those damn fools screwing up the atmosphere. Who the hell knows what they've done." The phone answers at the other end.

"Hey! We were just trying to get you," your daughter says in a quick playful voice. "Can you see it?" she asked excitedly.

"Hell yes we can see it. Where the hell is that idiot husband of yours? Why didn't he answer the phone?"

"We're going out," she answers back in a suddenly tired voice. "The trucks not running so he's getting the car from around back."

"Whose the hell idea was that?" The light around your body is extremely red and seems to be projecting in the direction of your daughter's house. "You don't know what this is. It could be some blast cloud from a bomb or something, those commie bastards. Stay the hell in the house till we get there."

"We won't be here. We're going..."

"John, I'm going back to bed. I can't take this," your wife says as she pulls the phone from your hand. "Listen to your father and stay in the damned trailer," she shouts into the receiver. Not waiting for a reply she slams the phone into place on the table.

The phone falls to the floor.

"Let's both go to bed," you say in as reassuring a voice as you can manage. Sexual feelings surge in your lower body. Taking her arm you gently guide her back to the bedroom, hoping this damn light stuff won't spoil your mood. Everything is drenched in glowing light; the clothes piled in the corner, the half dead plant hanging in the window, the magazines stacked against your night stand.

"Hey, I wonder if Miss July's cute little ass is glowing as brightly as yours," you grunt to your beloved as you bend over to pick up the latest issue.

"What a jerk," she snaps. "The damn place is on fire and all you can think of is looking at that young slut's ass." By her tone you know not to bother reaching over for a handfull.

"I'm sure she'd be happy to know it's you who's drooling over her pages," she jabs as she rolls onto her back, eyes closed, jaw clinched tight.

You imagine her closing every opening. "There's no penetrating you now," you mumble under your breath, secretly hoping she'll hear and be angry. She likes sex when she's angry. She gets a wild, uncontrollable look in her eyes.

You half roll your thick frame onto its side facing away from her anxious red mass of light. A gentle calm comes over you as you drift away, into a daze of scattered dissimilar thoughts. Calm. Seldom this calm.

Through half open eyes you catch a glimpse of sunlight pouring through the tear in the curtain. It creates a rainbow of colors as it streams across the room to its destiny on the wall. Unfamiliar feelings of beauty and wonder fill your mind as you stare endlessly into the glow. The painful realization that you have kept joy, beauty and awe from life presses against your heart, sending a hurt into your empty belly. With practiced skill you push the unwanted hurt feelings away. A flurry of confused sensations well up inside pushing the calm into panic. As soon as the panic grips it turns into calm. Now the calm becomes panic again. Laughter breaks the silence of the room as the next roller-coaster ride of feelings sends itself screaming through you. Sweat covers your body. Reeking smells of unclean body choke you awake. You look at the clock. Seven-forty-six. Images of the day ahead with all those lazy asses at work fills your head. Suddenly you're tired. You fight sleep, but it takes you into dreams of the struggles of the last several months, then years. You can feel time slipping away, but you can't wake up. It's as if you are sinking to a small place deep inside, away from all the uncertainty of your circumstances. Everything feels so distant, so far away.

The phone rings in the other room. You instantly know that it's your daughter. She's crying. It's like she's in your mind talking to you, pleading with you to help her. Struggling in a half dream, half real reality you manage to wade your heavy frame through the mess of light shooting up from the floor to the phone in the front room.

"I thought you were on your way over. You weren't answering so I thought.....I'm a little scared," she says in a little girl voice.

"Shit, what'd he do...I'll kick his..." you stop, knowing she knows the next few words by heart. Small feelings of meanness rip at you as you decide not to finish your threat against her husband.

"Tom's passed out on the sofa, Daddy. He keeps mumbling horrible things. I tried to wake him, but he just hits out at me. What's happening?"

"I'm a little out of it, Baby. I'm suppose to be at work. Shit, I'll get docked for this. You know how the boss man's been trying to fire me." Anger explodes in your chest. "Assholes everyone of them!" Your free hand grabs at the pain centered in your chest.

"Don't be mad, Daddy. Relax," your daughter pleads.

Calm comes too quickly. "I don't know what all this means. It's like every time I think of something it plays like a movie in my noggin." The top of your head feels cool as you rub your hand over the recently widening bald spot. It reminds you of your father. You push back tears. "Is it really bright over at the trailer?"

"Everything is glowing." There's a pause. "I feel okay. It doesn't hurt or anything. It's just Tom can't wake up. He got real mad when the car wouldn't start. He started throwing things at anything that moved, then fell unconscious on the steps. It was really weird. I drug him to the sofa," she says in a worried tone. "It's like he's been drinking, but he hasn't, honest."

The pause seems to clear the air. Suddenly you realize, every time you've spoken in the last ten minutes or so a spider web of gray glistening fibers hung in the air right in front of your face.

"No," you argue out loud, "It's more like they're wrapping themselves around...they're trying to choke me, but an invisible part of me is keeping them back." You rub the balding spot again. "Hell, it was like I could feel them getting tighter."

"Daddy!" your daughter shouts. "Stop it! You're talking like Tom."

"Huh?" The phone feels heavy in your hand. "I was just noticing things. You notice anything when you talk? It's like..."

"I'm okay." Her voice suddenly calm. "Is Mom okay?"

"She's out like a light in the bed," you say in a loud voice, hoping to scare away the webs. "You know how well she handles bad news."

"This isn't bad, and for some reason I feel happy about it glowing, whatever it is, even if Tom's passed out." Her voice seems fuller than yours. "I'm happ..."

"What the hell do you know," you shout, not liking the fact that she feels happy at something you can't understand. "Stay inside. Just do as I say and stay the hell inside." The phone breaks apart as it hits the wall.

From out of nowhere you feel angry at the world. "Screw work! Those bastards are always pulling me down. Screw her in the bed!" you yell through the walls separating the two of you. "You bitch, you always have to have it your way." You feel worn from the projections of resentment. "She takes all I got. Sucks me dry."

Images of a bad childhood flood your mind sending you back on the chair. Your father beating you for something you didn't do. Your mother out behind the back building kissing the man from down the street. His hand on her body. You playing with yourself as you watch him expose her large breasts. Memories of you watching her bathe; her catching you, then making you feel the wet hair between her legs. Pulling on your cock as you continue to watch them. Her mouth on him. Shuttering spasms spilling your fluids out on the ground. Scared and angry. Beating the dog with a hose. Feeling sorrow when it dies. Shame. Confusion about your feelings. Blame. Running away. Alone in the rain. Cold. Dark. Damn them! Wanting them to be looking for you. Hating them for hurting you.

The conflict ripping away at your body. Hatred blinding your sight. Deep belly pain doubling you over the back of the chair. Growing up hating everyone. Guilt about your own child. Being sexual with her. Deep shame at your excitement. Getting her to touch you the way her mother wouldn't. Feeling sick. Dying from the shame of knowing better and doing less.

Each dream worse than the last. Can't wake. Lost in the dream. Lost in the shame. Death tearing at your body. Cleansing your sins. Yes. Cleansing punishment. Fire burning away sin. Yes! Death!

The webs engulf your face blocking air from your lungs. Warm feelings you've never felt explode in your mind sending you upward toward a bright flash of light. A thunderous roar fills your head exploding each thought outward in every direction. A tunnel. Suddenly calm. Like never before. Never! Voices. Voices calling. Too dark to see. Looking into the darkness trying to see. People on both sides calling at you, pulling you over to the edge wanting you to take them with you. Hundreds of people shouting your name. Shadowy forms of dark colors standing staring at you. Smiling face. Pretty. Colorful. Bright. Sexual feelings pulling you to the side. Pleasure tearing at your calm. Burst of fluid spewing out of your genitals. You grasp at your body trying to hold back the flooding liquid. Dreams of them all. Roaring thunder clashing with light. Laughing lady face. Breast pushing hard against your face smothering life. You feel it leaving. Death. Cleansing death. More sexual urges. Burst of fluid spewing. Roaring thunder. Clashing light. Lost at the side. Lost in them pulling at you. Light above. Darkness below. Trapped. Can't move.

Again, how an individual responds during the first few days will be determined by his or her willingness to let go of conflict. The ancient prophets called this period, the time of judgment, when all men would be known by their manifesting thoughts. This is the time when each and every thought will be made manifest. If you remain fully conscious for the first three days, you will attain to self-realization and will know everything about everyone. Nothing will be withheld. Conflict is the only barrier. Conflict creates stress. Stress brings about disease. Disease manifests death.

Remember, it is not the conflict of the mundane everyday choices that plague us, but the conflict expressed in years of compromising our core beliefs to survive in a world that only honors those considered winners in the game of power.

THE FIRST THREE DAYS

"The great day of the Lord is near, near and hastening fast..."
The Book of Zephaniah 1: 14

To say that light will be coming from everywhere will be a mild understatement. By the end of the third day the Earth will appear to be as brilliant as any fusion star. This is the reason this event is referred to in the Akashic Records as the Twelve Days of Light. For twelve consecutive days the visible volume of energy emanating from the center of Creation will be such that the mundane spatial illusions of the collective mind will be eliminated as perception shifts to the fifth dimensional level of awareness.

Each and every human, without exception, will begin the Twelve Days fully aware that something very different is taking place. The primary differences in orientation will be cultural, with dogmatic religious beliefs confusing the greatest number. The God versus Devil, good versus evil, notions of the Abrahamic and Islamic movements will cause painful conflict internally and externally. Individuals within these religious cultures will turn to their respective clergy for guidance, but few will have anything to offer as a satisfactory explanation. Most will be in spiritual overwhelm themselves, having never really connected with the greater truths behind what they were teaching.

Education and socioeconomic levels will play a determining role, primarily because the poor and uneducated have almost no time to explore consciousness. And, this is about the willingness to let go of conflict, not the ability to win at the game of life. As a teacher once pointed out, "It can take up to five lifetimes to get over a good post-secondary education, and another ten to shake the effects of a private country club membership." As Buddha hinted, "It's the middle way – no attachment, no aversion."

The primary characteristics of the first three days are basically highlighted in scenario number one. There are a few details, however, that need further explanation, particularly the period between days three and four which are critical to certain events that will take place between days five and seven.

While this section is brief, it does contain important data for those remaining fully conscious for the duration of the full Twelve Days.

The First Day

Day one will have us seeing the world of physical matter like never before. Instead of the reflected light of the sun bouncing off molecules of matter, we will fully experience energy as it radiates out from the center of all substance. This is actually how the world looks to most of her creatures. So don't expect your pet to be overwhelmed by the astounding beauty along with you. We humans are the only animals that prefer the well defined edges of our illusionary vision. We do this mainly because it makes our everyday technological pursuits, our sciences and our arts, a little more manageable.

As the day progresses the light will intensify to clairvoyant proportions, giving each individual the opportunity to fully experience the texture and fabric of auric fields. Those who choose to remain conscious up to the end of the first day will also begin to realize just how much this world is about information. Everything will become multi-dimensional as awareness begins to shift from its third and fourth dimensional survival patterns to the creatively charged intelligence of third, fourth and fifth dimensional awareness. Color will have sound and odor; sound will radiate hue and fragrance; smells will carry tone and luminosity.

Our vision will be the most effected sense with everyone having a comparable experience just as they do now. Inanimate objects will radiate to four distinctive spectrums; objects of earth, such as minerals, will be dominantly yellow; water will radiate an overall white field; anything combusting will be a dazzling luminous red; the gases that make up our atmosphere will be a dazzling shimmering iridescent blue/green.

Human forms will be rainbow in effect with layers of color corre-

50

sponding to the seven central chakras. As an individual's awareness entertains a certain band of thought energy, a dominant field of color will overlay the seven layers of the aura causing them to appear even more luminous. This dominant field is an outward expression of our vitality and happens as we charge thought with emotional energy.

For individuals struggling with minor conflict and control issues during the Twelve Days, the shifts in this dominant field will seem wildly erratic. The repressed emotions of this and other lifetimes will release in waves of color as they review the unresolved immutable points of their incarnations. These individuals will appear to be struggling to stay alive, but the effect will remain primarily in the etheric body, leaving the physical body unharmed for the most part.

Those in profound conflict, such as the example in scenario number three, will more than likely die by the evening of the third day. The stress being generated by their conflict will further destroy the already damaged tissue of their organs. Individuals remaining fully conscious can alter the death effect of this group by lifting them out of their unconscious schizophrenia. These "saviors" will automatically know how to do this as they fully understand how loving compassion expands the energy of conflict into clarity.

Because animals have relatively stable emotional fields, and do not take the world personally, nor judge the validity of their existence, their auras are less likely to change dominant hues as they move through the day. It will appear as though nothing has changed in their reality. For them the world has always been a radiant place. The nine chakras in animals have similar colors to humans, so be prepared to apologize for not allowing your child to call the cat, "Rainbow." Animals do, however, charge thought with emotional energy, particularly if they are hunting. Also, the aura of a cat lying in the sun on the living room floor will shift as it dreams cat dreams, so there will be an opportunity to witness their moods.

It goes without saying, animals are influenced by humans. Because they often willingly take on the stress of their owners, it is important they be attended to during the first hours of day one. This stress could kill them as they progress through the Twelve Days. Each human/animal relationship develops its own distinct vocabulary of images and gestures. Even though it appears that all dogs communicate happy feelings by wagging their tails, happiness is not the only thing a wagging tail could mean. It is through compassionate understanding and the knowledge that animals are as much responsible for their circumstances as their owners, that owners will instinctively know how to effectively communicate with their animal companions. Animals see these relationships as equal in nature. Very few feel as though they actually own their humans. City dwelling animals will need to have certain plants available to help them stabilize, or at the very least, natural plant based remedies. (See the suggested reading section, *Treating Animal Illnesses and Emotional States with Flower Essence Remedies.*)

Small house plants give off hues of yellow at their roots, to purple then lavender at their tops regardless if they flower or not. Large plants layer much in the same way animals do, but the layers graduate in hues of the same dominant color instead of a rainbow configuration of many colors. You will be amazed at how animals, you being one, and plants communicate. Plants are deeply effected by animal auras and thought energy emotionally amplified by humans. If you were to stand in front of a budless flowering plant and emotionally charge a mental image of it blooming, you would be amazed at how fast it would begin to create a flower. Plants are also generators of emotional energy, producing a field of calming influence upon animals. As the Twelve Days progress, those remaining fully conscious will come to know how vital every green life form is to the continuation of all life upon the planet.

The most amazing plants in general will be large outdoor trees. The amount of consciousness concentrated in one tree will be difficult for most individuals to fully comprehend. Large trees have enormous tolerance for all forms of life. Maybe it is because of their long life spans, or the fact that they are rooted in one place and have developed tolerance as a means of survival. They are truly the royalty of this realm.

As you can imagine, the first day will be like a dream land of colors, smells and sounds. Uncontrollable waves of emotion are sure to threaten your stability as you witness the reality of this world for the first time in thousands of years. The most important thing you can do is to be with individuals of like mind. The natural high of being with those who know you will carry you through the critical period of the first two days.

The Second and Third Days

Colors, sounds and fragrances will reach their full intensity by the noon hour. Thoughts will begin to want to take immediate form early in the second day as thought energy begins to shift from expressing in the loosely formed energy waves we now experience to immediately actualizing as fields of substance. At first you will see this process as sparkles of light in the periphery of your vision. By the end of the third day every thought you entertain will manifest immediately.

This will be the dividing point for most of those individuals who want the old Picean system of thought, lag time, then manifest form, to remain. For them the experience of this shift to thought as substance will be actualized in what they think are dreams. Also, they have an investment in learning by rote, line upon line, etc. Eventually, even for the unconscious, learning though memorization or trial and error will be replaced with knowing. Those who go unconscious will do so because they will be operating from the notion that no one except God is to be all knowing.

By the end of the second day they will simply have too much information to easily handle from their frame of reference. They will choose to be unconscious. This presents a problem in that they will not make the paradigm shift consciously; as a result they will not consciously know they are fifth-dimensionally aware. After the Twelve Days have come and gone they will not be aware that they can operate from a fifth-dimensional state of being. Because of this they will try to impose the old system in the new, and will be allowed to do so for at least twenty-five years, up to 2026. At this time the collective mind will unify and even those who remained unconscious for the twenty-five years between 2001 and 2026 will be obliged to follow the new game plan for the next thirteen thousand years. A portion of that plan will be acted out here on Earth, then the collective mind will find a new dimensional world in which to play. The Akashic Records show human consciousness leaving the Earth in the year 6732 as we currently count. This is the last thirteen thousand year wave to affect human consciousness. It is because of this that the Earth is so populated. Everyone wants to be here on the surface, or at the very least, in the etheric body of the planet.

The third day will bring those remaining fully conscious into completion with all unresolved past issues, freeing them from the collective human mind, liberating them to the next level of Universal Mind. These individuals will retain all the abilities uncovered during the first three days. They will never be unconscious in a collective mind again.

The unconscious will continue a deep self-examination brought on by each thought manifesting in the moment. They will experience this as uncontrollably moving from dream to dream. This process will last until the tenth and eleventh days, with each individual coming up for air, and the occasional trip to the bathroom. Luckily the physical body is slave to habit and will act accordingly in sleep walking fashion.

Not all, but most of the profoundly conflicted will have dropped their bodies by this time. The etheric rifts and schisms created by their profound conflict and schizophrenic thoughts manifesting instantaneously around them will have been too much for their physical bodies to handle. Once dropping the physical body they will experience the balance of the Twelve Days in what would be described as hell, the lower astrals, having to face all their regretful deeds. They will move from nightmare to nightmare in an effort to cleanse themselves through punishment.

THE ASCENSION &
THE RAPTURE

"Then I looked, and lo, a white cloud, and seated on the cloud one like a son of man, with a golden crown on his head, and a sharp sickle in his hand. And another angel came out of the temple, calling with a loud voice to him who sat upon the cloud, 'Put in your sickle, and reap, for the hour to reap has come, for the harvest of the earth is fully ripe."
Revelation 14: 15

Between the third and fourth days, somewhere in the night, the first wave of ascension will take place. Fully conscious individuals who envision this as the next step for human awareness will return their physical bodies back to their original form – Light.

For some fifteen years now groups of individuals around the world have been actively studying the process of ascension. The modern idea of transfiguring the body back to light has its beginning approximately 2000 years ago. To many spiritual seekers ascension remains central to the promise of eternal life embodied in the demonstration given by Jesus. The good news: you don't have to be publicly humiliated then crucified to ascend.

The study of light body manifestation reaches back to ancient times and encompasses every new thought modality – from what to eat and how to prepare it, to when and how to breathe. For many, the pursuit of ascension has continued over hundreds of lifetimes. The group meditation, chanting, and emotional release work of the 70's and 80's is finding itself again in residential retreat centers specializing in teaching ascension techniques to those able to cough up the tuition, which in some cases is reported to be pretty hefty.

Some more good news: ascension happens in the moment one chooses to step out of the collective mind and return the physical body to light body expression. Enough have carried the torch through the generations since Atlantis to insure ascension as a choice in this end times. In other words, the idea of ascension is deeply placed in the collective mind. Because of this there is no ascension technique per say and there are some "prior to the moment" techniques that may help focus intention to that end. Everyone remaining fully conscious during the apexing of this thirteen thousand year energy event will know in the moment whether they will make that choice. Location, location, location is only important to merchants. No one geographical location is better than any other. Every place you step is hallowed ground.

The majority of those now studying ascension will leave Earth between days three and four returning in the year 2004 to excite the second wave of ascension that will last three years, ending in 2007. Most of the world's population will eventually leave Earth in this manner. However, the movement toward ascension will be relatively slow between 2007 and the final wave in 2011. The third and final wave of ascension signals the turning point for human consciousness as it relates to space and time.

Christians will see this as the promised rapture, the second coming of Christ.

Many mainstream Christians will find themselves in churches shortly after the first few hours of ground luminosity on day one of the Twelve Days. The bad news: most will be on their own as far as trying to answer the deeper questions of what is taking place in their world. The phrase most likely to be repeated over and over again will be the ever present, "The Lord works in mysterious way." Unholy ministers, particularly those who build financial monuments to themselves through the tithing of the fearfully faithful, know so little about the word of God, except, of course, when to quote scripture to prove their arguments. Their promise of salvation for money will be interestingly received on the other side. The good news is that those following these leaders will not suffer the same fate, and will more than likely find themselves ascending in the rapture they've heard so little about. This is His fulfillment to them. What a surprise to be face to face with the teacher they have loved for so long.

The true Christian mystics are on the fringe of the mainstream movement.

The much maligned charismatic and evangelical groups will gather together to be with their Lord and Savior, Jesus, and ascend en masse. They are aware of the coming events and have been presenting information about the end times so that the faithful will be prepared by knowing the signs. Their network of teachers and lay ministers will swing into high gear shortly after the first signs of the Twelve Days begin. To them this is the baptism by fire prophesied in Revelation. By the end of the third day all who say, "Lord, Lord," from the depth of their hearts, will be lifted into the Kingdom of God as described in Matthew 6: 2-8. Remember, every thought, all your deepest beliefs, will be made manifest by the end of the third day. For a great many Christians this will be the deep desire to be with their Lord and Savior.

The other major world religions will experience the events of the Twelve Days as the promise of their ancient prophets are at last fulfilled. Those attending the deeper mystical practices at the core of those religions will move into higher realms of being and knowing. Those sitting on the fence only giving lip service to the concepts of their faith will generate enough conflict to insure an unconscious state for the duration of the Twelve Days. The interesting thing is, fanatics, because they are not in conflict, will have a very direct experience of the Twelve Days and after the Twelve Days have gone will retain all the abilities of a fully enlightened fifth-dimensional individual.

DAYS FOUR, FIVE & SIX

"Then the seventh angel blew his trumpet, and there were loud voices in heaven, saying, 'The Kingdom of the world has become the Kingdom of God..."
Revelation 11: 15

For those not eating, sleeping or ascending, the fourth day will see a marked change in their perception of dimensional reality. Any continued feelings of conflict will have ended and judgement or comparison of any kind will have ceased by this point in awareness. All past and future focus is released in favor of the moment, the eternal now so often alluded to in mystical studies.

To remain fully conscious only requires the letting go of doubt and the ensuing conflict that it creates. Therefore, not everyone who remains fully conscious to this point will be operating from the ideals of enlightened leadership. Individuals who are without doubt, regardless of their beliefs, will be able to consciously manifest according to those beliefs. Many will be acting out deeply held religious beliefs, for instance, some will feel it their mission to save those choosing to continue in the unconscious state, particularly those still acting out the need to be cleansed through punishment as in scenario number three. Some of these savior types will directly intercede on the behalf of the unconscious in an attempt to quicken the unification of the collective mind. A high minded goal to say the least. However, the results of this action will vary according to each situation. The extreme result of awakening someone at this point would be to interrupt their process of completing with unresolved conflicts, sending them into a continued struggle that will last for many years. Interceding on behalf of loved ones or family members will be the most common effort of this activity.

Other saviors will act out of self interest, not at all working for the higher expression of liberating souls from the wheel of birth and death. They will intercede with this group to indenture them to particular belief systems. The vast majority of those choosing to go unconscious during the Twelve Days will be very happy to follow these dynamically charged individuals as they offer immediate solutions to life's little ups and downs after the Twelve Days have gone. This group will be ripe candidates for the fully conscious who are looking for followers. Matthew 7: 15 offers a very clear warning: "Be aware of false prophets, who come to you in sheep's clothing, but inwardly they are ravenous wolves." The cost of following is still the same price after the Twelve Days - your sovereignty.

There will also be those who feel it important to guide others to their way of thinking in an attempt to create community. Many of these individuals will be from the ranks of those who never quite felt as though they belonged here, either because they felt out of place with their culture or the present world values centered around consumption. These communities will be equivalent to the utopian communities that sprung up around the world in the late 1800's. These utopianists sought liberation from a world gone mad with power and greed. Imagine looking at the next fifty years on new year's eve of 1900. Global wars, global famine, global political and economical collapse, global natural disasters and last, but not least, global spiritual decline. In hindsight their desire to be out of the main stream might have been well founded – even if it meant living in the extremely austere circumstances of some of those communities. Having a community of like minded individuals to share a central focus will be of great value in the years 2001 through 2012. The shift from the old paradigm of the Picean Age to the new reality of the Aquarian Age will take its toll on the death and justice centered world culture. Fortunately for those of us not ascending, the toll will not be exacted in the same manner as the first fifty years of the twentieth century.

Another twist in the affairs of humankind will come from a very unique team of explorers. This group has been on the Earth for a very long time influencing and never directly interfering. Early in 2001, perhaps January, this cosmic band of aliens will announce their presence to the world. Ah, where would we be without CNN. They will finally come out of the cosmic closet primarily to offer a point of focus during the Twelve Days for those who have no religious faith or philosophy to guide their inquiry of this realm. The aliens understand how important it is in any realm to have a foundation of beliefs from which to project a vision of possibilities. It is the possibilities which set our sights. They will tell of knowing a continuous history that stretches back over one billion years. They will also tell of a Creator whose image is deeply etched in the soul of each conscious being. Western religions will balk at the notion of their description of an evolving God/Creator. Many of the religiously faithful will, even in light of overwhelming evidence, keep the creationist line. The alien's ideas of time and space will baffle most scientists who are bent on the present notions of physics. The fact that they have no need to rule or display power to force their ideas on those who do not wish to believe, will frustrate most world leaders. All in all, the world will be largely divided over their authenticity and intention. Soon after the Twelve Days, those who followed their suggestions will find themselves on ships headed for the home world of Suc'coth ben Oth, or simply, the Pleiadian system.

Day Five

Back to the subject – By this time the fully conscious will have grown accustomed to thought expressing as substance instead of energy and will carry on as though their real world were behaving like a dream. The difference being, they will experience the originating vortex forms, the spiraling energy patterns of etheric matter that bring physical substance into form. A crude example from our present reality might be being able to experience the outer surface of a painted wooden table, the surface of the wood the paint is adhered to, the fibers that compose the wood, the structures that create the fibers, the atoms that originate the sacred forms that manifest the structures of the fibers and the originating command that begins the process, all at the same time. They will also possess the ability to experience any individual layer as a focus of attention. Seems like a lot of information to the average mind. It is, and after the Twelve Days we will be anything but average. Physicists and

61

astrophysicists are aware of these other layers of reality right now. The only difference between then and now is the use of microscopes and telescopes as the means to experience. Those remaining fully conscious will function from Universal Mind and will be as the mystics have always been, able to experience all levels of manifest reality without any limitation. Space without time and absolute form.

Between Days Five and Six

As was stated earlier, mind, conscious awareness, is shifting from third and fourth-dimensional awareness to a dominant fifth-dimensional frame of reference. This shift in the vibrational frequency of the etheric body and its surrounding plasma field will cause a chain reaction in the deoxyribonucleic acid (DNA) of the physical body which stores, duplicates and passes on the information that makes life alive. The shift in the DNA will mutate all 46 chromosomes of the cell nuclei, shifting the backbone of alternating sugar and phosphate molecules along with the sugar molecules nitrogenous bases, interrupting the transmission of heredity patterns with this resulting effect: the physical body will not respond to genetic memory. The etheric body, with its seven energy centers called chakras, will become the operating organs. The organs of the physical body, with the exception of the heart, lungs and stomach, will gradually become as dormant as the glands of the endocrine system are now. Our need for external sustenance will no longer exist. The need for unconscious sleep will completely fall away. However, we will still breathe to attract chi from the etheric body of the planet to our physical bodies. Our hearts will pump fluid as a means of circulating the subtle chi energy that's vital to the connection between the etheric and physical bodies. We will also require water as a lubricant to the joints and connective tissue, to keep the skin and eyes moist and to replenish the fluids being pumped by the heart. Also, the etheric energy surrounding the molecules of water (H_2O) are needed to keep the electrical field of the physical body fully charged.

Because of this shift at the DNA level, our nervous systems will be able to handle the kundalini energy now dormant at the base of the spine. The upward expansion of this vertical Earth energy will awaken the profound force of the plasma field surrounding the etheric body giving unlimited physical powers to those who remain fully conscious during the Twelve Days. This plasma field is often mistaken for the light body, mainly because it appears as a shimmering body of light to those able to detect it, and it is this field of energy that allows the substance of the physical body to vibrate at the ascension level. This plasma effect will last indefinitely.

Day Six

Managing the effects of the leap from a limited organ based body dependent on the energies of the earth to survive, to an etheric body based on the subtle energies that abound in the universe, will take up most of the sixth day. Here is where each fully conscious individual gets to play with the reality of time and space as it relates to consciousness and energy. Time, or its nonexistence, will continue to be the most difficult aspect of the change to manage. Time will no longer be needed to accomplish any task, and because each thought is expressing as matter, tasks will not require outside resources.

At what level could you create with these new circumstances?

Imagine how Dilbert, the cartoon personality created by Scott Adams, would respond. No cubicle police. No more pointy haired bosses bottlenecking precious needs. Just himself and whoever and whatever he decides.

Anything is within the realm of possibility at this point. Imagination is the only boundary.

DAYS SEVEN, EIGHT & NINE

"The foundations of the wall of the city were adorned with every jewel; the first was jasper, the second sapphire, the third agate, the fourth emerald, the fifth onyx, the sixth carnelian, the seventh chrysolite, the eight beryl, the ninth topaz, the tenth chrysoprase, the eleventh jacinth, the twelfth amethyst. And the twelve gates were twelve pearls, each of the gates made of a single pearl, and the street of the city was pure gold, transparent as glass."
Revelation 21: 19

For the fully conscious, day seven will offer a few extra little bonuses. Life takes on dimensions not even previously imagined, as every soul's fragments, from all past, present and future incarnations, unify as One expressed being. Physical and etheric bodies, operating as one, will engender an unlimited feeling of generosity toward all of Creation. A profound alertness wrapped in a spacious calm permeates every moment, each breath is filled with divine enthusiasm for the joining of mastery with mystery, the absolute with the relative. Your senses will shift dramatically to an intuitive, clairvoyant range. A peachish gold hue will surround everything, eclipsing the aura and etheric body of any substance being observed. Gold flecks will radiate against the brilliant blue of our atmosphere as luminous flows of energy spiral outward to record each utterance in a manifest form. The song of the spheres will fill your heart as sound and color begin to blend into one expression, taking your observations into a multidimensional reality. Language will become useless as you realize no words can convey the full complexity of your conscious awareness. You will be able to penetrate the boundaries and layers of this world with mind sensations that combine fully formed thoughts with concise emotions. These condensed streams of consciousness laser beam along focused paths leading to a complete vision of the possibility within any consideration. You will express as a perfect concentration of body, mind and spirit. A whole within a whole, within One. True Trinity.

Quite a day, huh?

For those wanting to influence the less aware, the space between days six and eight is the perfect moment. Those choosing to be unconscious will be very receptive to any break in their process; they will grab at anything to help them awaken from their endless dreams. Their exhaustion will be exaggerated by the confusion of wanting to awaken, and being afraid to know. It is extremely important to be aware of your intention toward these individuals. The fact that you exist without conflict does not guarantee that your intervention will be received without conflict. Deep internal conflict in another tends to bring out the savior in those whose hearts are flung wide open, particularly if the individual in need is a loved one. The first four levels of love (see Notes section on page 87) can be very seductive even to an individual who has achieved the state of awareness afforded by the energies present from day seven onward.

At this point in the Revelation another phenomenon will be revealed to those not wishing to directly interfere with another's process. Any profound alteration in the consciousness of an individual will effect their genetic line in either direction for seven generations. In this approach, all we need to do is open ourselves to the possibility of love expressing as Creation. If we hold this to be true, then everyone around us will be dynamically effected by our internal spacious calm, with loved ones receiving the lion's share of renewed clarity. In other words, you awaken, others awaken. Sort of an instant hundreth monkey.

Day Eight

Another major shift in intention happens in the wee spaces of the eight day.

There will be a group of fully conscious individuals desirous of helping who will become centers of light and clarity for the unconscious. They will have gone beyond the need to express as savior and will be experienced as avatars, telepathically linked to one another.

It is out of their selfless desire to bring balance that they are able to heal even the greatest disease. The mission for them, therefore, will be to awaken as many souls as is possible, bringing them out of conflict into clarity of intention before the Twelve Days end. The importance of this can not be understated. This undertaking is to insure the balance of masculine/feminine awareness during the coming days of the one who will be called the Anti-Christ. Without this beginning balance in awareness the forces of skillful means would devastate wisdom; death would overcome life; the lust for power would eliminate grateful generosity. The good news: in the Akasha it is already written that this will be achieved.

Day Nine

The Twelve Days of Light is the line in the sand between the Piscean and the Aquarian Ages. Those wishing to continue Piscean beliefs will be allowed to do so until the year 2026. Everyone will be capable of fifth-dimensional awareness after day five, and it is because of this that they will be allowed to continue the concepts of duality and denial into the New Age. This is important to remember when reading the following material.

On day nine, there will be those who knowingly choose to offer the greatest demonstration in the years between 2003 and 2011. The complete vision of their martyrdom will be revealed. This is something they planned prior to their first breath in their first incarnation. These individuals know a great truth – to struggle against something is to make it real.

When these individuals are imprisoned and later asked to die, they will do so as an invocation to the highest world consciousness. In their allowed death they will bring forth the Great World Spirit spoken of in many native North American Indian prophecies. This invocation happens as a sacrifice because those souls choosing to release the body in full consciousness know of the alchemical effect this type of action has on the World Spirit. Each time a human gives its life in conscious choice, chi energy emanating out from the 144,000 physical cells of their soul matrix is released into the etheric body of the planet in a reverse, counter clockwise spin. The reverse spin draws the vertical energy of the Earth into itself, amplifying the original energy to such an intensity that it is able to be directed along multiple streams of consciousness, giving renewal to all forms of life.

On a greater scale, this amplified soul energy awakens the World Spirit who is then obligated to act on behalf of either those presiding over the energy event, such as a priest or magician, or the very souls who consciously released their physical bodies. In this case it will be the individual souls who will command the Great World Spirit. Their combined intention will be to bring a quick end to the inequities imposed against the meek by the one who will be called Anti-Christ.

DAYS TEN, ELEVEN & TWELVE

"Then he showed me the river of the water of life, bright as a crystal, flowing from the throne of God through the middle of the street of the city; also, on either side of the river, the tree of life with its twelve kinds of fruit..."
– Revelation 22

The last three days will be the reverse of the first three for the unconscious.

Many of those unconscious from day two to nine will gradually begin to awaken from their self imposed slumber on the tenth day. There will be a great deal of confusion and anger as they realize how much time they have spent unaware of the world around them. The memory of trying to awaken from unwanted dreams, of passing from one scenario of self examination to another, not being able to stop, will be fresh in their minds. Then there is the matter of explaining the missing loved ones and friends, those caught up in the rapture between days three and four. The frustration generated from the lack of reasonable explanations will be immense to say the least. The breakdown in the blind faith of those who have normally been good "followers" will be immediate and far reaching. Followers will want their leaders to know what has just transpired and the leaders will not know. Their lack of knowing will send the disillusioned toward the extraterrestrials who will have revealed themselves early in 2001 just for that reason.

For the unconscious who awaken during day twelve there will be a nagging sense of things not being right; a feeling of somehow being out of step with reality. The sensory effects of the Twelve Days – energy emanating from everywhere, thoughts manifesting as matter and the nagging sense that they are somehow greater than they believe themselves to be, will be very distracting while they try to put back the details of their lives.

It will be extremely easy for the early risers (days ten and early day eleven) to move into conscious fifth-dimensional awareness, that is, if they are lucky enough to have a fully conscious individual in their midst. If their attention is captured by those trying to save others, or someone who is playing out old Piscean control issues, they will slip back into the habits of the collective mind that existed prior to the Twelve Days.

The majority of those fully awakened during the Twelve Days will be completely alive expressing love in a most expansive manner. Their charity and compassion will only be eclipsed by their profound gratitude to Creator for all of life. They will see beyond the ordinary, looking deep into the souls of mankind. Their ability to bring wholeness to life will create them to be a great comfort to all who gather in their company. An infectious, ever expanding calm will be present wherever they go. The triple egg shaped concentric fields of blue luminous etherioplasmic energy (vaporous layers of manifest etheric substance similar to ectoplasm) surrounding their physical bodies will give them away as cosmically aware, compassionately driven individuals possessing abilities outside the natural range of perceptions for the collective mind. Only the unconscious who awaken by the close of day ten, or possibly early in day eleven will be able to recognize the etherioplasmic fields of those fully operating at fifth-dimensional level. After that, day twelve and on, the energy levels effecting the unconscious will be such as to generate a veiling effect across the etheric field of vision, disabling their ability to readily see auras or etherioplasmic bundles. This separation in abilities is self imposed and can be lifted at any moment as those late to awaken come to understand fifth-dimensional reality. This lifting of misunderstanding can also happen through a conscious teacher who is expressing expansive compassion.

The Eleventh Day

Each fully conscious individual will begin the manifestation of their particular aspect of the Aquarian vision of what is possible for human kind, just as those individuals did who remained fully conscious during the Atlantian Twelve Days. We only partially know of their abilities and manifest visions through the myths of Gods and Goddesses of ancient Greece and Rome. Unfortunately, we only have accounts of a few beings who had these God like powers. The majority chose to lead less obvious lives. Like them, the all knowing, completely sovereign individuals who remain fully conscious during the current Twelve Days will truly appear God like to anyone not operating at their level of awareness, intention and perception. It will be very annoying to the unconscious general public, just as it was annoying to the common ancient Greeks and Romans to have these interfering Titans running around altering perceptions of common reality.

Day Twelve

Here is where we, the collective mind and those who have moved out of the collective whole, cross the line in the sand separating the Piscean and Aquarian Ages. To quote a great individual of the Piscean Age, Martin Luther King, when he used the words of a wonderful gospel song, "Free at last. Free at last. Lord God Almighty, I'm free at last."

AFTER THE TWELVE DAYS

"And the city had no need of the sun or of the moon to shine in it, for the glory of God illuminated it..."
Revelation 21: 23

For those choosing to be unconscious, the Aquarian world after the Twelve Days will seem, for the most part, the same as the Piscean period they grew up in even though they are fully capable at any moment of expressing fifth-dimensional awareness. Actually, it is because of their fifth-dimensional capabilities that they are able to project Piscean beliefs into the Aquarian Age. Without this elevated ability to focus, they would be forced to experience this holy shift (the Twelve Days) fully exposed to the deep inner conflict creating their delusions of fear, shame and guilt. This could be devastating to the personality self which would then have to be repaired at an even higher level of Knowing.

Some of those who stay fully conscious during the Twelve Days might argue that full exposure to all personal delusions is the point and that less than complete self disclosure is delaying the collective process back to Unification. It is important to allow everyone their own unique path to self-realization. Staying fully conscious after the Twelve Days is extremely important, especially when it comes to the judgments of greater than and less than concepts. Just because an individual makes it through the shift fully conscious doesn't automatically mean they will remain self-realized after the intense energy of the Twelve Days has come and gone. It will be rare for someone who is realized to go unconscious after the Twelve Days, but it is not impossible. Thinking and acting out of judgment would be one way to achieve an unconscious state again.

The most confusing aspect of reality for those who went unconscious will be the lack of reasonable explanations as to what actually happened. Science will try to explain the missing twelve days as a mass hallucination brought about by some extraordinary field of energy our solar system passed through on its 25,000 year journey around galactic central sun. Western religious leaders will be embarrassed at their loss of any feasible explanation they can quote from the Bible. But instead of blaming Satan, they will focus their attention on the outside alien forces living on the planet. It will be interesting to watch these men of the cloth as they place blame on the Pleiadians and those from Orion. In doing so, they inadvertently authenticate the Pleiadian claims of being from outside our solar system, and therefore outside the immediate reach of the Genesis based creationist view.

As you can imagine, there will be any number of theories about the Twelve Days, but most will fall on deaf ears. People in general will really not want to know, they'll just want things to be the same as they were prior to all the craziness and confusion. It is because of this and the apparent lack of information concerning the visual phenomenons they experienced that it will only be a topic of conversation for a short period of time, say for a month or so, then the news services will be on to more pressing events, such as the sudden emergence of a world leader and the rapid movement toward the establishment of the "New World Order," one government, one new religion and one monetary system.

The truth is, no one will be able to effectively explain the mystery of the Twelve Days except those who remained fully conscious, but because most of them are not from the scientific or religious communities, they will be unofficial in their explanations, and in some cases, set aside as delusional. However, it will be difficult for those officiating to stave off those hungry for an explanation as to the missing days, let alone the vanished relatives and friends.

Something very important will be happening as human consciousness seeks a new level of normal as the days and weeks progress away from the twelve day energy event.

Earlier it was mentioned that the majority of those fully awakened will be expressing in profound compassion and expansive love. There will be those who are fully awakened who will seize the opportunity to control those who are less aware. Remember, the only condition that would bring about unconsciousness during the Twelve Days is conflict.

This needs to be restated here because most believers in the coming holy shift hold the belief that moving into fifth-dimensional awareness automatically means the expression of compassion and empowerment to others. It does not. In every age there are those who seek to save the world from itself. There will be a group of individuals who remain fully conscious during and after the Twelve Days who are operating from what could be considered the dark side – those wishing to control the destinies of others to bring about a better world for all. Remember, if you are without conflict concerning who you are, or what you are doing, then you will not go unconscious during the Twelve Days. Remaining awake has nothing to do with politics, religious beliefs or how you see yourself in relationship to the whole, unless those beliefs are creating inner conflict. These fully awakened individuals we are speaking of have no conflict about wanting to control the destinies of others because they truly see their role as saviors of the world. He who will be called the Anti-Christ will lead this group in his vision of what is possible for humanity. This Anti-Christ is the reincarnation of Belial, the last leader of Atlatia (Atlantis) and, Thoth, the creator of the early Egyptian culture.

Most of the population remaining unconscious during the Twelve Days (those hanging onto the old Piscean paradigm) will see the New World Order and its leader as dedicated to the advancement of global peace and cooperation. Unlike the United Nations, this organization will be effective in working with third world nations; so much so, that it will be viewed as being able to bring about miracles in all areas of life. These more mundane advancements will bring a real sense of purposefulness to the unawakened and in some cases will heal ancient hatreds kept alive by the general lack of affluent circumstances. Prosperity has a way of settling old disputes.

The individual who will become known as the Anti-Christ will actually begin to be present on the world scene in 1999. His ability to manipulate and control circumstances to desired outcomes is being tested in Mideastern political circles and he will gain even greater influence as he puts together what many will see as a lasting peace accord between the Jews and Arabs.

THE TWELVE DAYS OF LIGHT

Within this group several lesser leaders will be elected establishing a hierarchal structure of fifth-dimensional beings from which to command the activities of the new followers of Belial/Thoth. This will begin the final struggle of duality, prior to the Unification in 2026, as the forces loyal to Belial/Thoth begin to create their One World theme with its one spiritual view, one government, one goal – the eradication of individuated creative self expression. He who will be called the Anti-Christ sees his role as the One being who can bring about this concept of unification. His vision is for a unified world culture, but the greater reality of the Aquarian Age concerns unifying the collective mind in the unseen realms as well as in the physical universe.

From 2001 through to 2026 there will be a twenty-five year grace period, a time of adjustment, when both Piscean and Aquarian energies will be fully present. The jump from one age into the next would be too much for the collective mind without this period of overlapping energies. Even knowing this, it still seems odd that duality will take place at the fifth-dimensional level of awareness. Equally strange is the revelation in the Records that many who are presently well established on the side of sovereignty and compassion will join the ranks of this very charismatic leader of the New World Order. His expressed vision of a unified world with room for all life interrelating in a balanced order will be very persuasive. Unfortunately, the reality being inflicted upon people to create his vision will be far less than the vision itself. Then there is the matter of his abilities – he will be operating from sixth and seventh-dimensional awareness and seem light years ahead of everyone (including those who are cosmically aware) regarding solutions for everyday problems. He will be seen as a master, mainly because all his solutions will work <u>immediately</u>. There will be only one way to determine who he is – he will ask you to allow him to take care of your needs. Very simple and very appealing to many, especially those who still believe they must suffer to achieve. He will end their suffering. He will be seen as the savior of the world to these individuals, just as Jesus was seen as the messiah to the suffering of his time. This abnormal man from the Mideast, with his great expression of compassion will be seen as the answer to the world's ills. And he will be – for those who do not have visions of their own.

His minions will be very active and will enlist people before they know what happened. This new messiah will not tolerate those demonstrating fifth-dimensional awareness outside his ranks and will seek them out as trouble makers. This behavior is nothing new for those who seek to be the only expression of power. Absolute power, the power of life and death, is his personal agenda. He seeks to become an eternal being alongside Buddha, Esa, Kuthumi, Mohammed, and Quan Yin to name only a few.

The damning of the innocent will happen much the way it has happened throughout time – individuals demonstrating luminosity and boundless love will be presented as betrayers of the common path, out of step with the desires of the collective mind and will be taken out of view so as to not confuse the faithful followers. The meek, those operating out of compassion and expansive love, will not fight against those wishing to control their destinies. They understand that to fight against something, especially a belief, is to validate its existence and to lend it power. As a result of their passive, noncooperative stance, they will be isolated and brought together (between the years 2001 – 2011) for what will look like their imminent slaughter in the eyes of those who remained unconscious during the Twelve Days. This is not their end, but their complete empowerment. Because of their level of awareness and knowing, they can not be killed, nor can they be imprisoned, unless they want to for some greater demonstration, such as in the example of the crucifixion and resurrection of Jesus. They are essentially avatars, masters within this realm. Can you imagine what a problem they will be for those wanting to control? He who is to be called Anti-Christ will be deeply troubled by their presence, just as Herod was troubled by John the Baptist's constant voice. Please understand, the troubled feelings of the Anti-Christ are not conflict, per say, but the ancient notion that if you are not for someone or something, you are wholly against it. In this light you can bet the very existence of these avatars will be a profound threat to his vision of himself as Savior. With all these avatars running around, the general public might get the idea they do not need to be saved from themselves after all.

Interestingly, many who go unconscious during the Twelve Days, and become followers of Belial/Thoth, will begin to spontaneously awaken to fifth-dimensional awareness. They will do this as they become increasingly aware of the diminishing lag time between their desire and its manifest form. Because of this, they will begin to experience the magic of who they truly are. Eventually their numbers will be too great to allow for the strategy of removing all individuals expressing luminosity from the midst. By the year 2011 there will be sufficient numbers of Luminous beings on the planet to bring balance to the extreme measures being exerted by those working to control the destinies of others. The third wave of ascension in 2011 begins as a result of this balance in the duality. Many of those who left on the first ascension wave will return to demonstrate during the second wave which lasts from 2004 to 2007. Because this wave happens over a three year period it will not seem as dramatic or as concentrated as the first or third waves of ascension happening during the rapture or in 2011. The three waves of ascension are fulfillment of the prophecy.

There will be those individuals who, no matter what, will insist on imposing the conditions of the Piscean Age on the Aquarian Age right up until the end in the year 2026 when duality ends and the collective mind becomes One. These individuals are responding in this manner because of karmic issues that originate from their incarnations on the planet Maldec. That betrayal based karma is particularly difficult to release primarily because it involved so many innocent souls. (Information about Maldec can be found in, *"Other Tongues, Other Flesh,"* by George Hunt Williamson.)

Part of the vision the Anti-Christ has is a world free of strife. To this end he will actively fund all types of research. In 2004 a pharmaceutical company will develope a high density protein based on soy that will all but replace meat. Some people will still want their barbecue, but for the most part the world's population will be vegetarian. By the end of 2005 all the great waves of death that have plagued mankind, including cancer and AIDS, will be eliminated from the human experience. Early in 2006 all fossil, atomic and solar energy will be replaced by "free" energy in the form of cold fusion. By this time composite and ceramic materials will replace all metal and heavy plastics. At the same time biometal substances will become the new building materials due to their ability to be "grown" into any mold. Our need to launch free of the Earth's gravitational pull will be overcome when science discovers the laws of harmonic resonance as they relate to the consciousness of inanimate objects. Heavy objects being placed in orbit will ride up out of gravitational pull on a series of laser bursts. In a sense, this is the anti gravity technology science has been looking for. But first they have to discover that all matter is aware.

In the midst of all this technological advancement, humanity will finally remember that it <u>does</u> take an entire village to raise one child.

Another exciting development will be the end of time as it is now known to the collective mind. In other words, time will cease to exist. Just as the Earth was once thought to be flat, time will cease to be a limitation or a consideration for human consciousness. The Myans foretold this as happening on the winter solstice in the year 2012 and their prediction will be accurate for those choosing to be unconscious during days three through ten of the Twelve Days. (Time will have already ceased to be a factor for those who remain fully conscious during the Twelve Days.) Scholars have innocently interpreted the Myan prediction as meaning the end of the world and rightly questioned the validity of such a vision. The end of time is not the end of the world. Time is an invention of the intellect, not the other way around.

The Myans spiritual leaders worshiped time to the extent that they developed calendars of great accuracy to predict the coming cycles that were important to the lives of their people. To discount their knowledge of time and the cycles they projected into this current age would be extremely arrogant to say the least. In his book, *The Mayan Factor*, Jose Arguelles brings the story of this ancient people, a culture which possessed the ability to accurately predict the cyclical movements of distant celestial bodies. As a matter of fact, the Mayan's ability to tell time has only recently been surpassed by modern science with the invention of atomic clocks.

The Myans ability to predict celestial cycles was very important to their survival. The world of the last four hundred years has produced a different relationship with cycles and time. Time in relationship to movement has been a very important part of our exploration of this and other worlds. In the early days of global travel the element of time had to be discovered. Once an expedition returned, the amount of time it took to complete its voyage could be reported. To explore beyond Earth we must discover the amount of time it will take to complete a journey before embarking. This prior knowledge of duration is only necessary in a dimension where distance is calculated in terms of velocity, and in a dimension where velocity has an upward boundary such as the speed of light.

Since the advent of theoretical mathematics, science has pondered how to move beyond the speed of light. The speed of light question is our last major barrier to attaining liberation from our little blue marble of a home. If we jump beyond light, it is speculated, we can travel to other worlds. This is assuming, of course, that once we jump to beyond light, we can put on the brakes and jump back to the mundane velocities now hindering our migration into outer space. The shift from beyond light to sublight speed may be more devastating to molecular mass than the original jump to beyond light speed. We won't know unless we attempt it. You know that future saying, "Molecules, you can't live at light speed with them, and you can't live at sublight speed without them."

In the days immediately following the Twelve Days, scientists will begin to make profound discoveries about how time relates to space. Science fiction writers have given us a glimpse into the art of future travel and have even touched on the coming shift that will make space exploration truly possible – the theoretical wormhole. Scientists, in 2007, will finally get over themselves and discover a realm similar to ours existing as a continuum outside of the space/time/velocity conundrum. They will move forward cautiously not wanting to embarrass themselves or others with leaps in imagination. They will probe and ponder this sometimes only probable realm. (It seems only probable because it is not always immediately available to our physical senses.) Then, just as they get a handle on how to deal with these non specific space/time realities in relationship to the fragile human foil, time as the governing measure of velocity will be replaced by thought.

This will happen late in 2011. By December 22, 2012 the collective mind will step outside of time. Time will end.

Once the time/velocity question solves itself science will then turn to creating thought amplifiers just as they did in Atlantis some seventeen thousand five hundred years ago. These thought amplification modules will eventually power all external activities expressing in linear based sequential patterns such as the time based technologies we will chose to keep from the Piscean Age.

The next step will be to invent etherioplasmic forms capable of coexisting in the same immediate space with consciousness just as our awareness and physical bodies do now. Our present third and fourth-dimensional bodies are made up of atom based molecular matter. Our new bodies, being made of etherioplasmic substance, will respond to a greater range of influences instead of the limited range experienced by our solid, liquid and gas bodies. These new forms will be very elastic, giving greater latitude to consciousness as the dominant catalyst of shape and form. Our present molecular bodies exist both as genetic expressions and as projections of our subconscious beliefs. These new forms will express as conscious levels of intention. The immediate difference will be in our relationship with matter. For example, space will seem to fold, then unfold as we think (intend) ourselves into the next room. Teleportation. Telekineses. Telepathy. Where will it all end?

This getting up off our molecular masses will allow human awareness to inhabit bodies capable of holographically shifting within and between layered dimensional realities. Our present physical forms degenerate rapidly when encountering certain quantities and forms of radiation; and there is an enormous amount of radiation being generated in creation. There is also the phenomenon of gravity to contend with in our dense molecular forms. Traveling between the layers of dimensional reality is much easier to deal with than say the intense gravitational tug of a black hole. In our new forms the laws that govern our present physical bodies would not apply.

CONCLUSION

"They shall neither hunger anymore nor thirst anymore..."
Revelation 7: 16

What if all you have just read is true?

What if every thirteen thousand years we reinvent ourselves, alternating back and forth from unity to separation, forgetting the previous state in order to fully explore the present condition? What if this has been happening to past civilizations for millions of years? What if this is the last shift that will happen for human consciousness as we know it?

If all you have read here is true, then the game we've been playing is about to change dramatically. For those remaining fully conscious during the Twelve Days, the limitations of dimensional boundaries are about to dissolve into what may appear to be a limitless playground that responds to their every command. Are we about to know the other side of our nature – Co-creators in unity? We have certainly used the last thirteen thousand years to explore the many subtle layers of separation. Some would say that we waited to the last one hundred years to fully understand the true nature of duality and separation. Others might say that we had a greater sense of separation when each culture of the Earth was unaware of each other.

What ever the case, the door to the cage is about to be flung wide open. Many will leave Earth for adventures in other systems, others will stay to witness the Earth through her transition and healing. The "new" explorers from other systems who are currently incarnating into this paradigm will have the memory of separation and duality encoded in their souls as a way of preserving the living history of human consciousness in the Earth dimension as they move from one end of the unity/separation spectrum to the other over the next four thousand seven hundred and thirty-one years. The profound memory of separation will also serve to inspire them to keep a straight and narrow path toward greater unity as human consciousness prepares to leave this system in the year 6732. For those preparing for this next big shift, the good news

THE TWELVE DAYS OF LIGHT

is – the soul memory of unity you carry from the Lemurian/Atlantian period prior to last shift will be what inspires you to release the conflict of this period. Conflict, as was illustrated in the three scenarios, is the only hurdle to jump for any individual. The jump to fifth-dimensional awareness is not about how much an individual has learned or how well they have done, or not done. It is about the willingness to let go of conflict. Conflict remains the last barrier for everyone. Gratitude remains the salvation.

The only real question remaining is the problem with the manner in which the dates are reported in the Akashic Records. Now that the problem of which 2001 (Gregorian or actual), has been solved, we can get on with the question of the near identical sound symbols showing two different dates. Interestingly, this problem is peculiar to our generation, it does not happen for 1001 and 1011, nor does it happen at the one hundred year marks, such as 1901 and 1911. It is because of this that most clairvoyants interpret the dates as a window of opportunity for individuals to shift from third/fourth-dimensional awareness to third/fourth and fifth-dimensional awareness.

This window interpretation is understandable, but is easily dismissed in light of the amount of information in the Akasha concerning a singular event that effects the collective mind over a twelve day period as the apex point of a one thousand year energy event that cycles every thirteen thousand years. How are we to interpret this except as a singular collective event? And it is also true that each individual will have their own unique experience of the Twelve Days of Light, especially from day two onward. The wonderful thing is that the Twelve Days will begin in the same manner for everyone, no matter what the belief. No one will miss the beginning moments.

Another group of Akashic readers have suggested that the Twelve Days of Light will happen in 2011, with a ten year grace period beginning in 2001. They believe that the grace period will be used by the collective mind to cleanse itself of its conflict in preparation for the coming unity. Some from this group feel the ten year grace period is the coming apocalypse or period of tribulation described throughout the Bible. If this is true – that we must be completely cleansed of thousands of years of conflict – both individually and collectively, in a ten year period, then we are in for a very rough time. The Akasha indicates that the shift to fifth-dimensional awareness over a twenty-five year period, 2001-2026, is to be extremely confrontational to the collective mind. It would be hard to imagine what human consciousness would have to endure if the period between 2001 and 2011 is to be the period of purification. This could truly be the reign of terror described by Dante in his "Inferno."

No matter what scenario plays out, all who read the Akasha agree that the coming events are without doubt the grand moment of reckoning spoken of by the prophets, whose words are recorded in the Jewish Bible; and in the New Testament by John the Baptist; by Jesus and later by John the Beloved in his vision of Revelation; and in later works by Michel Nostradamus and by Edgar Cayce.

Another point the Akashic readers all agree on – how we enter this period individually and collectively will speak volumes about the true nature of our souls.

God/Goddess bless us all.

NOTES

Concerning race

The Akashic Records show little evidence of a racially pure people on the planet Earth. After all, most of us have in excess of thirty seven thousand ancestors. The genetically pure peoples are of indigenous decent, such as the Indians of North, Central and South America, several Black groupings in Africa, Ethiopia, and Australia, and Orientals in Tibet and China, and a small grouping of natives in Japan. The Records show the white race has been exploring the globe for some nine thousand years and by virtue of this has mixed will all the races.

The Akashic Records indicate the root race of all humans to be Black. After several genetic alterations orchestrated by our space brothers and sisters from the Pleiades, the Oriental race emerged from the Black and inhabited the Pacific basin. This 'new' race formed the civilization of Lemuria. After their experiment ended they moved up into the higher plateaus of western South, Central and North America. The civilizations of the Inca, Myan, Toltec, Aztec and Anazasi Indians are their descendants. The majority race in Atlantis, birth place of the early Egyptian culture, was a beautiful mixture of Black and Oriental.

After the break up of the Atlantian civilization thirteen thousand years ago, the survivors split into two groups. One went to Europe, the other to the east coast of North and South America, and the Caribbean islands. These individuals later joined with the Lemurian remnant that had moved up through Mexico and formed what we think of as the Red race.

With a little more genetic engineering from our space friends, the Black and Oriental mixture of Atlantis later became the Caucasian race that emerged in the Middle East in the Tigres and Euphrates River valleys. Around 10,000 BC the Caucasian race began mixing with the remnants of Atlantis. This mixture gave us the blood lines now prevalent in the Mid East. To further complicate the genetics of the Caucasians, the Oriental Tibetans moved into Europe and mixed with the whites to form the Slavic bloodlines of Northern Europe and Russia.

The Akashic Records show that the pure bloodlines are now dying out in favor of the mixed genetics of the 'new' races engineered with the help of aliens. This new race, a genetic blend of all the races, will be better able to withstand the coming etheric body (human) and atmospheric (planet) changes that are about to take place on the planet. The Records also show this new race will be the seed for the next great civilization to inhabit Earth. The previous race was of this planet. The new race will be of the stars.

Those who come back to earth for the next go-around that begins with a thousand years of peace, will have 4th & 5th dimensional etherial bodies. These new bodies will no longer suffer the limitations of the previous physical forms and will be able to move between dimensional realities much in the manner of the Lemurians. Reproduction will be etherial just as was in the Garden of Eden, or Lemuria.

Concerning the different levels of Love:
Part of the reason for our being here is to experience the core of the Collective Soul as it responds to the limitation boundaries of Earth Consciousness and its illusory presentation of matter to Human Consciousness. The Collective Soul is layered with ever expanding multidimensional forms which can best be described as feelings of Unlimited Love. As we explore this Soul, we move Consciousness through the levels of Love from instinctual Love, to Love that deprives, to Love that loves, to Love that forgives, to Love that nurtures, to Love that gives, to Love as Wisdom, to Love as unlimited Self Expression, to Love as Existence, and finally to Love as the personification of Creator.

Another interpretation of the term, Love, is Love as the Dynamic Singular Will forming Consciousness within Creation. Love by this definition is the unseen substance that permeates all matter. Still another definition has Love as the very Agency of our existence and one last definition has Love as the comforting Holy Spirit. When asked, each area of response within the Records shows one area of agreement relating to the subject of Love – little is known about Love beyond Love as Existence.

There are many teachers in this Earthly realm who are profoundly

88

qualified in this subject. When you are ready they will appear.

The following is for those wishing a more detailed definition of the levels of Love:

"Instinctual love" requires no special effort and is driven solely by the Law of Attraction. Usually those of a grouping, i.e., family, town, city, area, region, ethnic grouping, country, world, solar system, galaxy, universe, etc., will be in instinctual love.

"Love that deprives," is a self centered, manipulative force. We learn this Love as we embrace the illusion that we have to do something to get something, and that being right equals being Loved. The word "no" is often the trigger for the experience of deprivation. Also, this is the feeling of powerlessness experienced when one steps out of their instinctual grouping. Within our group we are understood; outside the group we have to explain ourselves.

"Love that loves" is based on Love toward an object for which one has a natural concern. "Love thy neighbor, as thy self." This is the love that bestows goodwill upon the recipient. Even though this is one of the most common forms of love, it is difficult to fully achieve.

"Love that forgives" as in the phrase, "Love thy enemy." This requires a great deal of tolerance and is extremely rare in Human Consciousness. This is a Love of intelligence and reason.

The "Love that nurtures" eventually is achieved by everyone. This is a love of great compassion. Here Human Consciousness expresses its true nature.

"Love that gives" without expectation. This is well beyond the understanding of most humans. The score card has been dropped in favor of being a Source for those in the illusion of need. This is the Selfless Self.

"Love as Wisdom" is the joining of the heart and head. At this level the need to be right has all but disappeared, and thought is in perfect communion with feeling. This level is seldom reached by the unenlightened.

"Love as Unlimited Self-Expression." This is you expressing as a full sovereign Being, manipulating the illusions of this world through the power found within their limitations.

"Love as existence," and "Love as the personification of Creator God" speak for themselves.

Where is the collective mind on this scale?

To use these definitions as a scale of judgment as to where you or the Collective are in the progression toward Self-Realization would be an inappropriate use of this information. The levels of Love outlined are all expressing here on the planet or we would be unaware of them. And, there are more than likely other levels elsewhere. Here are some milestones from the Abrahamic religions: Solomon was a demonstration of Love as Wisdom; Moses expressed Love as the personification of Creator God; Jeshua Ben Joseph (Jesus) was expressing Love as Forgiveness and Love as Existence. And these from other cultures: Buddha demonstrated Love as Existence and Love as the personification of Creator God; Quan Yin was the expression of the Love that Nurtures and Love as Existence; Confucius demonstrated Love as Wisdom; Mohammed exampled Love as the personification of Creator God. There have been many others from all the world's cultures and religions who have achieved these levels of Love. One hundred forty four thousand to be exact. History, as it is chronicled by mankind, has missed the journeys of most of these individuals.

From The First Book of Moses called,

Genesis:
Chapter One

1. In the beginning God created the heavens and the earth. 2. The earth was without form, and void; and darkness was upon the face of the deep; and the Spirit of God was moving over the face of the waters. 3. And God said, Let there be light; and there was light. 4. And God saw that the light was good; and God separated the light from darkness. 5. God called the light Day, and the darkness he called Night. And there was evening and there was morning, one day.

6. And God said, "Let there be a firmament in the midst of the waters, and let it divide the waters from the waters." 7. And God made the firmament, and separated the waters which were under the firmament from the waters which were above the firmament. And it was so. 8. And God called the firmament Heaven. And there was evening and there was morning, a second day.

9. And God said, "Let the waters under heaven be gathered together into one place, let the dry land appear." And it was so. 10. God called the dry land Earth; and the waters that were gathered together He called Seas. And God saw it was good. 11. And God said, "Let the earth put forth vegetation, plants yielding seed, and the fruit trees bearing fruit in which is their seed, each according to its kind, upon the earth. And it was so. 12. The earth brought forth vegetation, plants yielding seed according to their own kinds, and trees bearing fruit in which is their seed, each according to its kind: and God saw that it was good. 13. And there was evening and there was morning, a third day.

14. And God said, "Let there be lights in the firmament of the heaven to separate the day from the night; and let them be for signs and for seasons, and for days, and for years: 15. And let them be lights in the firmament of the heavens to give light upon the earth." And it was so. 16. And God made the two great lights; the greater light to rule the day, and the lesser light to rule the night: he made the stars also. 17. And God set them in the firmament of the heaven to give light upon the

earth, 18. And to rule over the day and over the night, and to separate the light from the darkness: and God saw that it was good. 19. And there was evening and there was morning, a fourth day.

20. And God said, "Let the waters bring forth swarms of living creatures, and let birds fly above the earth across the firmament of heavens. 21. And God created great whales, and every living creature that moves, which the waters brought forth abundantly, after their kind, and every winged fowl after his kind: and God saw that it was good. 22. And God blessed them, saying, "Be fruitful, and multiply, and fill the waters in the seas, and let fowl multiply in the earth". 23. And there was evening and there was morning, a fifth day.

24. And God said, "Let the earth bring forth the living creature after his kind: cattle, and creeping thing, and beast of the earth after his kind. And it was so. 25. God made the beast of the earth according to their kinds, and cattle according to their kinds, and everything that creeps upon the earth after his kind. And God saw that it was good.

26. Then God said, "Let us make man in our image, after our likeness: and let them have dominion over the fish of the sea, and over the fowl of the air, and over the cattle, and over all the earth, and over every creeping thing that creeps upon the earth." 27. So God created man in his own image, in the image of God created he him; male and female created he them. 28. And God blessed them, and God said upon them, "Be fruitful, and multiply, and replenish the earth, and subdue it: and have dominion over the fish of the sea, and over the fowl of the air, and over every living thing that moves upon the earth." 29. And God said, "Behold, I have given you every plant bearing seed, which is upon the face of all the earth, and every tree with seed in its fruit; you shall have them for food. 30. And to every beast of the earth, and to every fowl of the air, and to every thing that creeps upon the earth, wherein there is life, I have given every green plant for food." And it was so. 31. God saw every thing that he had made, and behold, it was very good. And there was evening and there was morning, a sixth day.

Chapter Two

1. Thus the heavens and the earth were finished, and all the host of them. 2. And on the seventh day God finished his work which he had done; and he rested on the seventh day from all his work which he had done. 3. So God blessed the seventh day, and hallowed it, because on it God rested from all his work which he had done in creation.

4. These are the generations of the heavens and the earth when they were created, 5. when no plant of the field was yet in the earth, and there was no man to till the ground; 6. but a mist went up from the earth, and watered the whole face of the ground. 7 then the Lord God formed man of dust from the ground, and breathed into his nostrils the breath of life; and man became a living being. 8. And the Lord God planted a garden in Eden, in the east; and there he put the man whom he had formed. 9. And out of the ground the Lord God made to grow every tree that is pleasant to the sight, and good for food, the tree of life also in the midst of the garden, and the tree of the knowledge of good and evil.

10. A river flowed out of Eden to water the garden; and there it divided, and became four rivers. 11. The name of the first is Pishon; it is the one which flows around the whole land of Hav'i-lah, where there is gold; 12. and the gold of that land is good; bdellium and onyx stone are there. 13. the name of the second river is Gihon; it is one which flows around the whole land of Cush. 14. And the name of the third river is Hid'-ke-kel, which flows east of Assyria. And the fourth river is the Euphra'-tes.

15. The Lord God took the man, and put him in the garden of Eden to till it and keep it. 16. And the Lord God commanded the man saying, "You may freely eat of every tree of the garden; 17. but of the tree of the knowledge of good and evil you shalt not eat, for in the day that you eat of it you shall die."

18. Then the Lord God said, It is not good that the man should be alone; I will make him a helper fit for him." 19. So out of the ground the Lord God formed every beast of the field, and every bird of the air; and brought them to the man to see what he would call them; and whatever the man called every living creature, that was its name. 20.

The man gave names to all cattle, and to the fowl of the air, and to every beast of the field; but for the man there was not found a helper fit for him. 21. So the Lord God caused a deep sleep to fall upon Adam, and while he slept took one of his ribs and closed up its place with flesh. 22. And the rib, which the Lord God had taken from man, he made into a woman and brought her unto the man. 23. And Adam said,

"This at last is bone of my bones, and flesh of my flesh: she shall be called Woman, because she was taken out of Man."

24. Therefore a man leave his father and his mother and cleaves unto his wife: and they become one flesh.

25. And the man and his wife were both naked, and were not ashamed.

Chapter Three

Now the serpent was more subtle than any other wild creature that the Lord God had made. He said to the woman, "Did God say, 'You shall not eat of any tree of the garden'?" 2. And the woman said to the serpent, "We may eat of the fruit of the trees of the garden; 3. but God said, 'You shall not eat of the fruit of the tree which is in the midst of the garden, neither shall you touch it, lest you die.'" 4. But the serpent said to the woman, "You will not die. 5. For God knows that when you eat of it your eyes will be opened, and you will be like God, knowing good and evil." 6. So when the woman saw that the tree was good for food, and that it was a delight to the eyes, and that the tree was to be desired to make one wise, she took of its fruit and ate; and she also gave some to her husband, and he ate. 7. Then the eyes of both were opened, and they knew that they were naked; and they sewed fig leaves together and made themselves aprons.

8. And they heard the sound of the Lord God walking in the garden in the cool of the day, and the man and his wife hid themselves from the presence of the Lord God among the trees of the garden. 9. But the Lord God called to the man, and said to him, "Where are you?" 10. And he said, "I heard the sound of thee in the garden, and I was afraid, because I was naked; and I hid myself." 11. He said, "Who told you that you were naked? Have you eaten of the tree of which I com-

manded you not to eat?" 12. The man said," The woman whom thou gave to be with me, she gave me fruit of the tree, and I ate." 13. Then the Lord God said to the woman, "What is this that you have done?" The woman said, "The serpent beguiled me, and I ate." 14. The Lord God said to the serpent,

"Because you have done this, cursed are you above all cattle, and above all wild animals; upon your belly you shall go, and dust you shall eat all the days of your life.

15. I will put enmity between you and the woman, and between your seed and her seed; and he shall bruise your head, and you shall bruise his heel."

16. To the woman he said, "I will greatly multiply your pain in child bearing; in pain you shall bring forth children, yet your desire shall be for your husband, and he shall rule over you."

17. And to Adam he said, "Because you have listened to the voice of your wife, and have eaten of the tree of which I commanded you, 'You shall not eat of it,' cursed is the ground because of you; in toil you shall eat of it all the days of your life;

18. thorns and thistles it shall bring forth to you; and you shall eat the plants of the field.

19. In the sweat of your face you shall eat bread till you return to the ground, for out of it you were taken; you are dust, and to dust you shall return."

20. The man called his wife's name Eve, because she was the mother of all living. 21 And the Lord God made for Adam and his wife garments of skins, and clothed them.

22. Then the Lord God said, "Behold, the man has become like one of us, knowing good and evil; and now, lest he put forth his hand and take also of the tree of life, and eat, and live for ever'- 23. therefore the Lord God sent him forth from the garden of Eden, to till the ground from which he was taken. 24. He drove out the man; and at the east of the garden of Eden he placed the cherubim, and a flaming sword which turned every way, to guard the way to the tree of life.

SUGGESTED READING

Very few books written are devoted exclusively to the subject of the millennium shift. And there are many works that include information or prophecy concerning the collective shift to more expanded realms of awareness. Part of my joy in researching this book was the adventure of diving into the ideas of others. Many of the authors listed have numerous titles.

Arguelles, Jose. *The Mayan Factor Path Beyond Technology.* Santa Fe: Bear & Company, 1987

Alexander, Thea. *2150 AD.* New York: Batam Books, 1979

Bachofen, J. J. *Myth, Religion & Mother Right.* Princeton: Bollingen Series/Princeton University Press, 1967

Bacon, Sir Francis. *The History of Winds.* London, 1671

Baigent, Michael & Richard Leigh. *The Dead Sea Scrolls Deception.* New York: Simon & Schuster, 1991

Bailey, Alice. *Esoteric Psychology.* Lucis Publishing Company

Bulfinch, Thomas. *Myths of Greece and Rome.* New York: Penguin Books, 1981

Campbell, Joseph (with Bill Moyers). *The Power of Myth.* New York: Doubleday, 1988

Cayce, Edgar. *Edgar Cayce on Atlantis.* New York: Warner Books, 1988

Cottrell, Leonard. *The Lost Pharaohs.* New York: Grosset & Dunlap, 1961

Drummond, Henry. *Natural Law in the Spiritual World.* New York, 1883

Dyer, Dr. Wayne. *Real Magic.* New York: Happer-Collins, 1993

Einstein, Albert. *The World as I See It.* New York: Citadel Press, 1995

Eisenman, Robert & Michael Wise. *Dead Sea Scrolls Uncovered.* New York: Penquin Books, 1992

Fix, Wm. R. *Pyramid Odyssey.* Urbanna, VI: Mercury Media Books, 1984

Fortune, Dion. *The Mystical Qabalah.* York Beach, Maine: Samuel Weiser, 1984

Hall, Manly P. *The Secret Teachings of All Ages*. Los Angles: The Philosophical Research Society, Inc., 1989

Hawking, Stephen W. *A Brief History of Time*. New York: Bantam Books, 1988

Hogue, John. *Nostradamus & The Millennium*. New York: Double Day -Dolphin, 1987

Holy Bible. Revised Standard Version. New York: Thomas Nelson & Sons, 1953

Jarno, Trudy. *The New Millenium: Under the Cosmic Influence of the Outer Planetary Systems*. Santa Monica: Dennis-Landman, 1992

Lacarriere, Jacques. *The Gnostics*. San Francisco: City Lights Books, 1989

Nada-Yolanda. *Evolution of Man*. Miami: Mark Age Period & Programs, 1971

On Mankind Their Origin and Destiny. London, 1872

Pagels, Elaine. *The Gnostic Gospels*. New York: Vintage Books, 1979

Roberts, Jane. *The Seth Materials*.

---. *Seth Speaks*.

---. *The True Nature of Reality*.

Robinson, James M. *The Nag Hammadi Library*. San Francisco: Harper Collins, 1990

Rosenfield, Israel. *The Strange, Familiar and Forgotten*. New York: Alfred A. Knopf, 1992

Sheldrake, Rupert. *The New Science of Life: The Hypothesis of Morphic Resonance*. Rochester, Vermont: Park Street Press, 1995

Starhawk. *The Spiral Dance, a Rebirth of the Ancient Religion of the Great Goddess*. New York: Harper & Row, 1979

Talbot, Michael. *The Holographic Universe*. New York: Harper Perennial, 1991

von Daniken, Erich. The Eyes of the Sphinx. New York: Berkley Books, 1996

Williamson, George Hunt. *Other Tongues – Other Flesh*. Albuquerque: Be Books,1954;

——. *Secret Places of the Lion*. Rochester, Vermont: Destiny Books, 1958

Wolf, Fred Alan. *Parallel Universes*. New York: Simon & Schuster, 1988

Order Form

Fax Orders: 404 874-5892   **Telephone Orders:** 800 871-4996
e-Mail: RRose8@mindspring.com   **Web:** www.richmanrose.com
Postal Orders: Richman Rose Publishing
                       Post Office Box 7766
                       Atlanta, Georgia 30357-0766

Please send the following books or products:
I understand that all tapes are guaranteed and will be replaced if defective.

YOUR BOOK of LIFE Accessing the Akashic Records   192 pages paperback,
Bibliography, index.   15.95 x ___ + $4.00 ea. S&H* = $_____

Accessing the Akashic Records $15 x ___ + $3.50 ea. S&H* = $_____
2 tape set. Introduction on side A, guided meditations on sides B, C & D

Accessing Your Book of Life $15 x ___ + $3.50 ea. S&H* = $_____
2 tape set. Introduction on side A, guided meditations on sides B, C & D

THE TWELVE DAYS of LIGHT – Prophecy Concerning the Millenium
112 pages paperback   10.95 x ___ + $4.00 ea. S&H* = $_____

                                        Sub Total: $_____

Sales tax: Georgia residents add applicable sales tax. $_____

Shipping: $ _____
  *If ordering more than one item, add .75 S&H for each additional item.
        Call for next day or second day air delivery cost.

                                        Total: $ _____

Payment: ☐ Credit Card   ☐ Check payable to Richman Rose Publishing
               Name on card:_____
               Card number:_____ Exp. Date: /

Send to: Name_____
               Address _____
               City/State_____Zip_____